Wide Angle

OXFORD
UNIVERSITY PRESS

JENNIFER CARLSON

OXFORD
UNIVERSITY PRESS

198 Madison Avenue
New York, NY 10016 USA

Great Clarendon Street, Oxford, OX2 6DP,
United Kingdom

Oxford University Press is a department of the University of Oxford. It furthers
the University's objective of excellence in research, scholarship, and education by
publishing worldwide. Oxford is a registered trade mark of Oxford University Press
in the UK and in certain other countries

ISBN: 978 0 19 452860 3   1 Wide Angle American 1 SB W/OP Pack
ISBN: 978 0 19 452836 8   1 Wide Angle American 1 SB
ISBN: 978 0 19 454669 0   1 Wide Angle American 1 OP

Printed in China

This book is printed on paper from certified and well-managed sources

ACKNOWLEDGEMENTS

Back cover photograph: Oxford University Press building/David Fisher

Illustrations by: 5W Infographics pp. 31, 35, 37, 38, 48, 110, 155; Ricardo Bessa/Folio
Illustration Agency p. 84; Stuart Bradford p. 64; Martin Hargreaves/Illustration
Web p. 20; John Holcroft/Lindgren & Smith pp. 86, 105; John Jay pp. 53, 93; Arunas
Kacinska/Eye Candy Illustration pp. 22, 148; Michael Kirkham/Heart USA Inc pp.
14, 16, 43; Shaw Nielsen pp. 13, 25, 37, 49, 61, 73, 85, 97, 109, 121, 133, 145; Greg
Paprocki p. 100.

Video Stills: Mannic Productions: pp. 12, 24, 36, 48, 60, 72, 84, 96, 108, 120, 132, 144.
Oxford University Press: pp. 29, 82,100. People's Television: pp. 50, 130.

*The Publishers would like to thank the following for their kind permission to reproduce
photographs and other copyright material*: **123rf:** pp. 4 (coffee beans/Somsak
Sudthangtum), 38 (castle/Peter Mocsonoky), 55 (4/Goran Bogicevic), 76 (3/
luckybusiness), 80 (parachuting /Natalia Klenova), 103 (chair/jedendva), (table/
Andrew Mayovskyy), 116 (hotel on water/Tatiana Popova), 136 (b/Nenad Aksic), (h/
alexiakhruscheva), 142 (Optimist/racorn), 149 (2/Nuttakit Sukjaroensuk), (4/Andre
Bonn), (8/Eray Haciosmanoglu), 154 (jeans/chiyacat), (shirt/Olga Popova), (t-shirt/
Kanstantsin Prymachuk), 158 (3/visionsi); **Alamy:** pp. 4 (Apple Mac/Kalyan Boruah),
(cotton/Boaz Rottem), (Mariachi trumpeter/Barry Lewis), (soccer ball/John Baran),
(Volkswagen Beetle/imageBROKER), 10 (3/keith morris), (4/Hero Images Inc.), (6/
Rafe Swan), (8/Sue Andrews), 11 (5/WENN), (6/dpa picture alliance), (8/dpa picture
alliance), 13 (shaking hands/Tetra Images), 17 (frame/Jozef Polc), (game/Andor
Bujdoso), (tickets/ITAR-TASS Photo Agency), 19 (2/Tom Wood), (5/Cultura Creative
(RF)), (8 frame/Sophie McAulay), 22 (interviewer/PjrTravel), 28 (4/Blend Images), (6/
Alex Segre), (7/p. forsberg), 34 (house exterior/Matthew D. White/VWPics), 41 (Little
Women/INTERFOTO/History), 44 (coffee smile/EYESITE), 47 (night/Image Source),
(park/Givaga), 52 (1/Ira Berger), (5/Aurora Photos), (7/Global Warming Images), (8/
Patti McConville), 54 (traffic/David Wall), 55 (1/Prisma by Dukas Presseagentur
GmbH), (3/format4), 66 (bat/WILDLIFE GmbH), (Daniel Kish/ZUMA Press, Inc.), (Tori
Allen/Aurora Photos), 67 (3/Phanie), (4/Viacheslav Iakobchuk), 68 (amusement
park/Maciej Bledowski), (dog/Johner Images), 70 (Avicenna/Everett Collection),
(Ben Franklin/Wim Wiskerke), 76 (4/__David Gee), (5/Blend Images), 80 (Amelia

Earhart/Pictorial Press Ltd), (Valentina Tereshkova/SPUTNIK), 88 (Burj Al Arab/
imageBROKER), (Cesar Ritz/Paul Fearn), (Ritz Hotel exterior/Ian Shaw), 88-89 (Ritz
Hotel interior/Imagedoc), 102 (camping/imageBROKER), (bed/Zoonar GmbH),
(refrigerator/Vladislav Kochelaevskiy), 108 (mac and cheese/Brent Hofacker),
(steak & kidney pie/numb), 112 (1/Gary A Nelson/Dembinsky Photo Associates), (3/
robertharding), (8/George H.H. Huey), 113 (garden/Alex Arnold), 115 (cave paintings
Juxtlahuaca/Danita Delimont), (man/Doug Blane/Extreme Sports Photography),
116 (castle/LOOK Die Bildagentur der Fotografen GmbH), 117 (Mary/Blend Images),
118 (village/Tonellophotography), 122 (hotel and pool/TNT Magazine), (Sahara/
blickwinkel), 124 (game on screen/Cigdem Simsek), 127 (student/Hero Images Inc.),
129 (music lesson/Hero Images Inc.), (scientist/Hero Images Inc.), 134 (shaking
hands/LJSphotography), 136 (c/MBI), (d/Robin Beckham/BEEPstock), (f/BSIP SA), 139
(candles/Ruth Black), 143 (a/Ian Allenden), (b/Image Source), (c/Dmitriy Shironosov),
152 (Michael Phelps/dpa picture alliance archive), 158 (1/Gallo Images), (6/YAY
Media AS); **Bank of England:** p. 4 (£20 note/Bank of England); **Blink:** Cover,
Photo Illustration by Krisanne Johnson, pp. 3 (1 opener/ Krisanne Johnson), 9 (chef/
Nadia Shira Cohen), 15 (2 opener/Edu Bayer), 26 (gift/Quinn Ryan Mattingly), 27 (3
opener/Quinn Ryan Mattingly), 33 (Peru/Edu Bayer), 39 (4 opener/ Edu Bayer), 45
(playing soccer/Quinn Ryan Mattingly), 51 (5 opener/Krisanne Johnson), 59 (woman
on bike/Nadia Shira Cohen), 63 (6 opener/Krisanne Johnson), 65 (street performer/
Nadia Shira Cohen), 75 (7 opener/Gianni Cipriano), 82 (charity/Krisanne Johnson),
87 (8 opener/Gianni Cipriano), 95 (fashion/Krisanne Johnson), 99 (9 opener/Nadia
Shira Cohen), 104 (vacation/Edu Bayer), 111 (10 opener/Gianni Cipriano), 117 (Tiber
river/ Gianni Cipriano), 123 (11 opener/Edu Bayer), 125 (fashion designers/Gianni
Cipriano), 135 (12 opener/Quinn Ryan Mattingly), 141 (party/Gianni Cipriano);
Getty: pp. 4 (pretzel/dallosto), 5 (Karim/Jetta Productions), 10 (1/Aping Vision/STS),
(2/Christian Liewig - Corbis), 11 (1/Jeremy Sutton-Hibbert), (2/Joe Robbins), 13 (kids
and parent/Image Source), (women greeting/Heinrich van den Berg), 28 (2/Geber86),
34 (French Quarter/Toby Adamson), 46 (Ray Rich/Stephen Simpson Inc), 57 (Family
meal/Lucy Lambriex), 66 (Stephen Wiltshire/Dan Kitwood), 70 (DaVinci/DEA/D.
DAGLI ORTI), 76 (01-Jan/Radius Images), 77 (boy at window/laflor), 98 (Hicham El
Guerrouj/Michael Steele), 102 (glamping/Leslie WEST), (treehouse glamping/John
Warburton-Lee), 108 (bubble and squeak/Jonathan Lovekin), 112 (6/Dennis Barnes),
(7/Jonathan Kingston), 114 (underwater cave/Giordano Cipriani), 115 (cave paintings
Altamira/Print Collector), 116 (scary house/Pete Ryan), 118 (hotel on water/M
Swiet Productions), 126 (doughnuts/Martine Mouchy), (fashion school/Portra
Images), 136 (e/Roy JAMES Shakespeare), 137 (chariot racing/Dorling Kindersley),
(Circus Maximus/Heritage Images), 142 (Pessimist/Caiaimage/John Wildgoose), 147
(Patrick McGoohan/Popperfoto), 156 (Oscar Wilde/Alfred Ellis & Walery/Stringer);
iStock: p. xvi, (phone/lvcandy), (tablet/RekaReka); **NASA:** p. 81 (Apollo 11 crew/
NASA); **OUP:** pp. 47 (sunrise/slhy), 88 (Taj Mahal/Mazzzur), 112 (2/JeniFoto); **REX:**
p. 11 (3/REX/Shutterstock); **Shutterstock:** pp. 4 ('sol de Mayo' symbol/ASUWAN
MASAE), (bull/lberto clemares exposito), (flamenco guitartist/Anastasia Vavilina),
(Mini Cooper/Grisha Bruev), (Mount Fuji/Aeypix), (pato player/sunsinger), (phone/
Nebojsa Markovic), (pyramid/sculpies), (Seoul Tower/leungchopan), (tacos/
zoryanchik), (Tokyo/Blue Planet Studio), (US $/Anton Watman), 5 (Hanna and Emilia/
racorn), (Kalto/leungchopan), (Marlana /antoniodiaz), 7 (chef/wavebreakmedia), 10
(5/LightField Studios), (9/urbazon), (10/DnDavis), 11 (4/Frederic Legrand - COMEO),
(7/Daniel Hurlimann), 13 (men greeting/antoniodiaz), 14 (woman/Blend Images), 17
(bags/Basak Zeynep congur), (balloons/Business stock), (colouring/ivan_kislitsin), 19
(1/ermess), (3/AntartStock), (4/AntartStock), (6/Egyptian Studio), (7/think4photop), (8
flower/Riegler Klaus), 20 (Alexander Graham Bell /Everett Historical), 28 (1/Capricorn
Studio), (3/Rawpixel.com), (5/Iakov Filimonov), (8/IlkerErgun), 29 (British Airways/
VanderWolf Images), 32 (Salford Quays/Gordon Bell), 38 (Helsingor/RPBaiao),
40 (family/Monkey Business Images), 52 (2/Michael715), (3/Gertjan Hooijer), (4/
frank_peters), (6/wavebreakmedia), 55 (2/Andrey Yurlov), (5/Iakov Filimonov),
(6/India Picture), 67 (1/Fresnel), (2/wavebreakmedia), (5/The Magical Lab), (6/
OSORIOartist), 68 (Amira/Nicoleta Ionescu), (tea/digieye), 76 (2/baranq), 77 (male
friends/Syda Productions), (playing in snow/Lucky Business), (raining/CK Ma), 88
(Great Wall /Hung Chung Chih), 91 (family/antoniodiaz), 101 (mac and cheese/Igor
Dutina), 103 (desk/Artbox), (lamp/Stockforlife), (sofa/bluehand), (TV/Ksander), 110
(café/Africa Studio), 112 (4/Andrey Kotov), (5/mRGB), 114 (cave/Aleshin_Aleksei),
116 (forest adventure/ER_09), 117 (Amir/Tatiana Frank), (Austria/Evgeniya
Anikienko), (Malcolm/elix Mizioznikov), (Sofia/Eugenio Marongiu), 118 (bin bags/
donvictorio), 122 (snow cave/Budkov Denis), 124 (game designer/mirtmirt), 126
(gym/MilanMarkovic78), 127 (cooking/Arina P Habich), (museum/Popova Valeriya),
129 (selfie/Claudia K), 130 (bored/Monkey Business Images), 136 (a/Rawpixel.com),
(g/Dmytro Zinkevych), 137 (gladiators/rudall30), 148 (moon/vovan), 149 (1/Seeme),
(3/M. Ali Khan), (5/VladKol), (6/Pressmaster), (7/vilax), 154 (dress/Tarzhanova), (jacket/
gogoiso), (skirt/gogoiso), 158 (2/Studio Romantic), 158 (4/Oleksandra Naumenko), (5/
ognennaja); **Superstock:** p. 10 (7/Caia Images/Caia Images).

Authentic Content Provided by Oxford Reference

The author and publisher are grateful to those who have given permission to reproduce the following extracts and adaptations or copyright material:

p.5 Adapted from *A Guide to Countries of the World* edited by Christopher Riches and Peter Stalker. Oxford University Press, 2016. http://www.oxfordreference.com/view/10.1093/acref/9780191803000.001.0001/acref-9780191803000

p.20 Adapted from "Bell, Alexander Graham" in *The Oxford Companion to British History* edited by Robert Crowcroft and John Cannon. Oxford University Press, 2015. http://www.oxfordreference.com/view/10.1093/acref/9780199677832.001.0001/acref-9780199677832-e-421

p.33 Adapted from "Cuzco" in *The Oxford Companion to Archaeology* edited by Neil Asher Silberman. Oxford University Press, 2012. http://www.oxfordreference.com/view/10.1093/acref/9780199735785.001.0001/acref-9780199735785-e-0110

p.41 Adapted from "Little Women" in *The Oxford Companion to American Literature* edited by James D. Hart and Phillip W. Leininger. Oxford University Press, 1995. http://www.oxfordreference.com/view/10.1093/acref/9780195065480.001.0001/acref-9780195065480-e-2827

p.80 Adapted from "Earhart, Amelia" in *The Oxford Encyclopedia of Women in World History* edited by Bonnie G. Smith. Oxford University Press, 2008. http://www.oxfordreference.com/view/10.1093/acref/9780195148909.001.0001/acref-9780195148909-e-279

p.80 Adapted from "Tereshkova, Valentina" in *The Oxford Encyclopedia of Women in World History* edited by Bonnie G. Smith. Oxford University Press, 2008. http://www.oxfordreference.com/view/10.1093/acref/9780195148909.001.0001/acref-9780195148909-e-1064

p.98 Adapted from "four-minute mile" in *A Dictionary of Sports Studies* edited by Alan Tomlinson. Oxford University Press, 2010. http://www.oxfordreference.com/view/10.1093/acref/9780199213818.001.0001/acref-9780199213818-e-494

p.101 Adapted from "Comfort Food" in *The Oxford Encyclopedia of Food and Drink in America* edited by Andrew F. Smith. Oxford University Press, 2012. http://www.oxfordreference.com/view/10.1093/acref/9780199734962.001.0001/acref-9780199734962-e-1064

p.115 Adapted from "Juxtlahuaca Cave, Guerrero, Mexico" in *The Concise Oxford Dictionary of Archaeology* edited by Timothy Darvill. 22 Nov. 2017. http://www.oxfordreference.com/view/10.1093/oi/authority.20110803100027887

p.115 Adapted from "Altamira, Spain" in *The Concise Oxford Dictionary of Archaeology* edited by Timothy Darvill. Oxford University Press, 2008. http://www.oxfordreference.com/view/10.1093/acref/9780199534043.001.0001/acref-9780199534043-e-115

p.128 Adapted from "learning styles" in *A Dictionary of Education* edited by Susan Wallace. Oxford University Press, 2015. http://www.oxfordreference.com/view/10.1093/acref/9780199679393.001.0001/acref-9780199679393-e-549

p.137 Adapted from "Circus Maximus" in *A Dictionary of Sports Studies* edited by Alan Tomlinson. Oxford University Press, 2010. http://www.oxfordreference.com/view/10.1093/acref/9780199213818.001.0001/acref-9780199213818-e-227

p.147 Adapted from "The Self" in *Oxford Essential Quotations* edited by Susan Ratcliffe. Oxford University Press, 2017. http://www.oxfordreference.com/view/10.1093/acref/9780191843730.001.0001/q-oro-ed5-00009264

p.148 Adapted from "Buddy De Sylva 1895–1950 and Lew Brown 1893–1958" in *Oxford Dictionary of Modern Quotations* edited by Elizabeth Knowles. Oxford University Press, 2008. http://www.oxfordreference.com/view/10.1093/acref/9780199208951.001.0001/q-author-00005-00000479

p.149 Adapted from "J. H. Payne" in *Oxford Essential Quotations* edited by Susan Ratcliffe. Oxford University Press, 2017. http://www.oxfordreference.com/view/10.1093/acref/9780191843730.001.0001/q-oro-ed5-00008225

p.150 Adapted from "Amos Bronson Alcott" in *Oxford Essential Quotations* edited by Susan Ratcliffe. Oxford University Press, 2017. http://www.oxfordreference.com/view/10.1093/acref/9780191843730.001.0001/q-oro-ed5-00011946

p.151 Adapted from "Travel and Exploration" in *Oxford Dictionary of Humorous Quotations* edited by Gyles Brandreth. Oxford University Press, 2013. http://www.oxfordreference.com/view/10.1093/acref/9780199681365.001.0001/q-subject-00008-00000286

p.152 Adapted from "Michael Phelps" in *Oxford Essential Quotations* edited by Susan Ratcliffe. Oxford University Press, 2017. http://www.oxfordreference.com/view/10.1093/acref/9780191843730.001.0001/q-oro-ed5-00008298

p.153 Adapted from "Michelle Obama" in *Oxford Essential Quotations* edited by Susan Ratcliffe. Oxford University Press, 2017. http://www.oxfordreference.com/view/10.1093/acref/9780191843730.001.0001/q-oro-ed5-00016286

p.154 Adapted from "L.P. Hartley" in *Oxford Dictionary of Quotations* edited by Elizabeth Knowles. Oxford University Press, 2014. http://www.oxfordreference.com/view/10.1093/acref/9780199668700.001.0001/q-author-00010-00001523

p.155 Adapted from "Houses" in *Oxford Essential Quotations* edited by Susan Ratcliffe. Oxford University Press, 2017. http://www.oxfordreference.com/view/10.1093/acref/9780191843730.001.0001/q-oro-ed5-00005620

p.156 Adapted from "Gossip" in *Oxford Essential Quotations* edited by Susan Ratcliffe. Oxford University Press, 2017. http://www.oxfordreference.com/view/10.1093/acref/9780191843730.001.0001/q-oro-ed5-00004973

p.157 Adapted from "Malala Yousafzai" in *Oxford Essential Quotations* edited by Susan Ratcliffe. Oxford University Press, 2017. http://www.oxfordreference.com/view/10.1093/acref/9780191843730.001.0001/q-oro-ed5-00017266

p.158 Adapted from "Philander Chase Johnson" in *Oxford Dictionary of Quotations* edited by Elizabeth Knowles. Oxford University Press, 2014. http://www.oxfordreference.com/view/10.1093/acref/9780199668700.001.0001/q-author-00010-00001781

Cover photo by Krisanne Johnson.
Cape Town, South Africa, January 2017.
Young adults practice with their dance troupe before the start of a neighborhood parade in Mitchell's Plain during the Cape Town Minstrel Carnival season in Cape Town, South Africa. The carnival's history dates back to slave traditions during the days of the Cape Colony, when slaves were given a day off on January 2nd each year. Troupes begin the day's festivities by parading through the main streets of different neighborhoods in the Cape Flats.

Contents

ENGLISH FOR REAL	GRAMMAR	VOCABULARY	PRONUNCIATION	REVIEW
▶ Greetings and introductions	The verb *be*: Positive and subject pronouns Questions with *be* *Be*: Negative	Nationalities Jobs	Sounds of the alphabet	see page 147
▶ Being polite to strangers	Singular and plural nouns Demonstrative adjectives and pronouns Possessive *'s* and possessive adjectives	Numbers 21-101 Adjectives Personal items	Pronouncing numbers	see page 148
▶ Giving directions	*There is…* and *There are…* Imperatives (commands) *There is/There are*: *Yes/no* questions and negative statements	Places in a town Prepositions of place Rooms in a house	Weak sound of *are* in *there are*	see page 149
▶ Asking for the time	Simple present Simple present: *Yes/no* questions Simple present: Negative forms	Family Habit/Routine verbs Prepositions of time: *in*, *on*, *at*	/s/, /z/, /ɪz/ in simple present verbs	see page 150
▶ Asking someone to repeat something	Adverbs of frequency *like/love/hate* + a verb in the *-ing* form The simple present: *wh-* questions	Transportation Travel (verbs) Word building: *-er* and *-ist* (*traveler, cyclist*)	Falling intonation in *wh-* questions	see page 151
▶ Keeping the conversation going	*can/can't* for ability Adverbs of manner *Yes/no* questions with *can*	Abilities (verbs) Sports and activities Adjective + *at* + noun	*Can/can't* for ability	see page 152

v

Acknowledgments

AUTHOR

Jennifer Carlson holds a BA in Comparative Literature in English, German, and Spanish from the University of Massachusetts at Amherst. As a VISTA volunteer, she coordinated an ESL program for immigrants and refugees, and she has taught ESL/EFL in the United States and Mexico. She has been working in academic publishing for nearly two decades, more than half of which has been spent developing and writing content for Spanish and English language learning.

SERIES CONSULTANTS

PRAGMATICS **Carsten Roever** is Associate Professor in Applied Linguistics at the University of Melbourne, Australia. He was trained as a TESOL teacher and holds a PhD in Second Language Acquisition from the University of Hawai'i at Manoa. His research interests include interlanguage pragmatics, language testing, and conversation analysis.

Naoko Taguchi is an Associate Professor of Japanese and Second Language Acquisition at the Dietrich College of Modern Languages at Carnegie Mellon University. She holds a PhD from Northern Arizona University. Her primary research interests include pragmatics in Second Language Acquisition, second language education, and classroom-based research.

PRONUNCIATION **Tamara Jones** is an instructor at the English Language Center at Howard Community College in Columbia, Maryland.

INCLUSIVITY & CRITICAL THINKING **Lara Ravitch** is a senior instructor and the Intensive English Program Coordinator of the American English Institute at the University of Oregon.

ENGLISH FOR REAL VIDEOS **Pamela Vittorio** acquired a BA in English/Theater from SUNY Geneseo and is an ABD PhD in Middle Eastern Studies with an MA in Middle Eastern Literature and Languages from NYU. She also designs ESL curriculum, materials, and English language assessment tools for publishing companies and academic institutions.

MIDDLE EAST ADVISORY BOARD **Amina Saif Al Hashami**, Nizwa College of Applied Sciences, Oman; **Karen Caldwell**, Higher Colleges of Technology, Ras Al Khaimah, UAE; **Chaker Ali Mhamdi**, Buraimi University College, Oman.

LATIN AMERICA ADVISORY BOARD **Reinaldo Hernández**, Duoc, Chile; **Mauricio Miraglia**, Universidad Tecnológica de Chile INACAP, Chile; **Aideé Damián Rodríguez**, Tecnológico de Monterrey, Mexico; **Adriana Recke Duhart**, Universidad Anáhuac, Mexico; **Inés Campos**, Centro de Idiomas, Cesar Vallejo University, Peru.

SPAIN ADVISORY BOARD **Alison Alonso**, EOI Luarca, Spain; **Juan Ramón Bautista Liébana**, EOI Rivas, Spain; **Ruth Pattison**, EOI, Spain; **David Silles McLaney**, EOI Majadahonda, Spain.

We would like to acknowledge the educators from around the world who participated in the development and review of this series:

ASIA Ralph Baker, Chuo University, Japan; **Elizabeth Belcour**, Chongshin University, South Korea; **Mark Benton**, Kobe Shoin Women's University, Japan; **Jon Berry**, Kyonggi University, South Korea; **Stephen Lyall Clarke**, Vietnam-US English Training Service Centers, Vietnam; **Edo Forsythe**, Hirosaki Gakuin University, Japan; **Clifford Gibson**, Dokkyo University, Japan; **Michelle Johnson**, Nihon University, Japan; **Stephan Johnson**, Rikkyo University, Japan; **Nicholas Kemp**, Kyushu International University, Japan; **Brendyn Lane**, Core Language School, Japan; **Annaliese Mackintosh**, Kyonggi University, South Korea; **Keith Milling**, Yonsei University, Korea; **Chau Ngoc Minh Nguyen**, Vietnam – USA Society English Training Service Center, Vietnam; **Yongjun Park**, Sangi University, South Korea; **Scott Schafer**, Inha University, South Korea; **Dennis Schumacher**, Cheongju University, South Korea; **Jenay Seymour**, Hongik University, South Korea; **Joseph Staples**, Shinshu University, Japan; **Greg Stapleton**, YBM Education Inc. – Adult Academies Division, South Korea; **Le Tuam Vu**, Tan True High School, Vietnam; **Ben Underwood**, Kugenuma High School, Japan; **Quyen Vuong**, VUS English Center, Vietnam

EUROPE Marta Alonso Jerez, Mainfor Formación, Spain; **Pilar Álvarez Polvorinos**, EOI San Blas, Spain; **Peter Anderson**, Anderson House, Italy; **Ana Anglés Esquinas**, First Class Idiomes i Formació, Spain; **Keith Appleby**, CET Services, Spain; **Isabel Arranz**, CULM Universidad de Zaragoza, Spain; **Jesus Baena**, EOI Alcalá de Guadaira, Spain; **José Gabriel Barbero Férnández**, EOI de Burgos, Spain; **Carlos Bibi Fernandez**, EIO de Madrid-Ciudad Lineal, Spain; **Alex Bishop**, IH Madrid, Spain; **Nathan Leopold Blackshaw**, CCI, Italy; **Olga Bel Blesa**, EOI, Spain; **Antoinette Breutel**, Academia Language School, Switzerland; **Angel Francisco Briones Barco**, EOI Fuenlabrada, Spain; **Ida Brucciani**, Pisa University, Italy; **Julie Bystrytska**, Profi-Lingua, Poland; **Raul Cabezali**, EOI Alcala de Guadaira, Spain; **Milena Cacko-Kozera**, Profi-Lingua, Poland; **Elena Calviño**, EOI Pontevedra, Spain; **Alex Cameron**, The English House, Spain; **Rosa Cano Vallese**, EOI Prat Llobregate, Spain; **Montse Cañada**, EOI Barcelona, Spain; **Elisabetta Carraro**, We.Co Translate, Italy; **Joaquim Andres Casamiquela**, Escola Oficial d'Idiomes – Guinardó, Spain; **Lara Ros Castillo**, Aula Campus, Spain; **Patricia Cervera Cottrell**, Centro de Idiomas White, Spain; **Sally Christopher**, Parkway S.I., Spain; **Marianne Clark**, The English Oak Tree Academy, Spain; **Helen Collins**, ELI, Spain; **María José Conde Torrado**, EOI Ferrol, Spain; **Ana Maria Costachi**, Centro de Estudios Ana Costachi S.I., Spain; **Michael Cotton**, Modern English Study Centre, Italy; **Pedro Cunado Placer**, English World, Spain; **Sarah Dague**, Universidad Carlos III, Spain; **María Pilar Delgado**, Big Ben School, Spain; **Ashley Renee Dentremont Matthäus**, Carl-Schurz Haus, Deutch-Amerikanisches-Institute Freiburg e.V., Germany; **Mary Dewhirst**, Cambridge English Systems, Spain; **Hanna Dobrzycka**, Advantage, Poland; **Laura Dolla**, E.F.E. Laura Dolla, Spain; **Paul Doncaster**, Taliesin Idiomes, Spain; **Marek Doskocz**, Lingwista Sp. z o.o., Poland; **Fiona Dunbar**, ELI Málaga, Spain; **Anna Dunin-Bzdak**, Military University of Technology, Poland; **Robin Evers**, l'Università di Modena e Reggio Emilia, Italy; **Yolanda Fernandez**, EOI, Spain; **Dolores Fernández Gavela**, EOI Gijón, Spain; **Mgr. Tomáš Fišer**, English Academy, Czech Republic; **Juan Fondón**, EOI de Langreo, Spain; **Carmen Forns**, Centro Universitario de Lenguas Modernas, Spain; **Ángela Fraga**, EOI de Ferrol, Spain; **Beatriz Freire**, Servicio de Idiomas FGULL, Spain; **Alena Fridrichova**, Palacky University in Olomouc, Faculty of Science, Department of Foreign Languages, Czech Republic, **Elena Friedrich**, Palacky University, **JM Galarza**, Iruñanko Hizkuntz Eskola, Spain; **Nancie Gantenbein**, TLC-IH, Switzerland; **Gema García**, EOI, Spain; **Maria Jose Garcia Ferrer**, EOI Moratalaz, Spain; **Josefa García González**, EOI Málaga, Spain; **Maria García Hermosa**, EOI, Spain; **Jane Gelder**, The British Institute of Florence, Italy; **Aleksandra Gelner**, ELC Katowice, Bankowa 14, Poland; **Marga Gesto**, EOI Ferrol, Spain; **Juan Gil**, EOI Maria Moliner, Spain; **Eva Gil Cepero**, EOI La Laguna, Spain; **Alan Giverin**, Today School, Spain; **Tomas Gomez**, EOI Segovia, Spain; **Mónica González**, EOI Carlos V, Spain; **Elena González Diaz**, EOI, Spain; **Steve Goodman**, Language Campus, Spain; **Katy Gorman**, Study Sulmona, Italy; **Edmund Green**, The British Institute of Florence, Italy; **Elvira Guerrero**, GO! English Granada, Spain; **Lauren Hale**, The British Institute of Florence, Italy; **Maria Jose Hernandez**, EOI de Salou, Spain; **Chris Hermann**, Hermann Brown English Language Centre, Spain; **Robert Holmes**, Holmes English, Czech Republic; **José Ramón Horrillo**, EOI de Aracena, Spain; **Laura Izquierdo**, Univerisity of Zaragoza, Spain; **Marcin Jaśkiewicz**, British School Żoliborz, Poland; **Mojmír Jurák**, Albi – jazyková škola, Czech Republic; **Eva Kejdová**, BLC, Czech Republic; **Turlough Kelleher**, British Council, Callaghan School of English, Spain; **Janina Knight**, Advantage Learners, Spain; **Ewa Kowalik**, English Point Radom, Poland; **Monika Krawczuk**, Wyższa Szkoła Finansów i Zarządzania, Poland; **Milica Krisan**, Agentura Parole, Czech Republic; **Jędrzej Kucharski**, Profi-lingua, Poland; **V. Lagunilla**, EOI San Blas, Spain; **Antonio Lara Davila**, EOI La Laguna, Spain; **Ana Lecubarri**, EOI Aviles, Spain; **Lesley Lee**, Exit Language Center, Spain; **Jessica Lewis**, Lewis Academy, Spain; **Alice Llopas**, EOI Estepa, Spain; **Angela Lloyd**, SRH Hochschule Berlin, Germany; **Helena Lohrová**, University of South Bohemia, Faculty of Philosophy, Czech Republic; **Elena López Luengo**, EOI Alcalá de Henares, Spain; **Karen Lord**, Cambridge House, Spain; **Carmen Loriente Duran**, EOI Rio Vero, Spain; **Alfonso Luengo**, EOI Jesús Maestro Madrid, Spain; **Virginia Lyons**, VLEC, Spain; **Anna Łętowska-Mickiewicz**, University of Warsaw, Poland; **Ewa Malesa**, Uniwersytet SWPS, Poland; **Klara Małowiecka**, University of Warsaw, Poland; **Dott. Ssa Kim Manzi**, Università degli Studi della Tuscia – DISTU – Viterbo, Italy; **James Martin**, St. James Language Center, Spain; **Ana Martin Arista**, EOI Tarazona, Spain; **Irene Martín Gago**, NEC, Spain; **Marga Martínez**, ESIC Idiomas Valencia, Spain; **Kenny McDonnell**, McDonnell English Services S.I., Spain; **Anne Mellon**, EEOI Motilla del Palacar, Spain; **Miguel Ángel Meroño**, EOI Cartagena, Spain; **Joanna Merta**, Lingua Nova, Poland; **Victoria Mollejo**, EOI San Blas-Madrid, Spain; **Rebecca Moon**, La Janda Language Services, Spain; **Anna Morales Puigicerver**, EOI TERRASSA, Spain; **Jesús Moreno**, Centro de Lenguas Modernas, Universidad de Zaragoza, Spain;

ix

Emilio Moreno Prieto, EOI Albacete, Spain; **Daniel Muñoz Bravo**, Big Ben Center, Spain; **Heike Mülder**, In-House Englishtraining, Germany; **Alexandra Netea**, Albany School of English, Cordoba, Spain; **Christine M. Neubert**, Intercultural Communication, Germany; **Ignasi Nuez**, The King's Corner, Spain; **Guadalupe Núñez Barredo**, EOI de Ponferrada, Spain; **Monika Olizarowicz-Strygner**, XXII LO z OD im. Jose Marti, Poland; **A. Panter**, Oxford School of English, Italy; **Vanessa Jayne Parvin**, British School Florence, Italy; **Rachel Payne**, Academia Caledonian, Cadiz, Spain; **Olga Pelaez**, EOI Palencia, Spain; **Claudia Pellegrini**, Klubschule Migros, Switzerland; **Arantxa Pérez**, EOI Tudela, Spain; **Montse Pérez**, EOI Zamora, Spain; **Esther Pérez**, EOI Soria, Spain; **Rubén Pérez Montesinos**, EOI San Fernando de Henares, Spain; **Joss Pinches**, Servicio de Lenguas Modernas, Universidad de Huelva, Spain; **Katerina Pitrova**, FLCM TBU in Zlin, Czech Republic; **Erica Pivesso**, Komalingua, Spain; **Eva Plechackova**, Langfor CZ, Czech Republic; **Jesús Porras Santana**, JPS English School, Spain; **Adolfo Prieto**, EOI Albacete, Spain; **Sara Prieto**, Universidad Católica de Murcia, Spain; **Penelope Prodromou**, Universitá Roma Tre, Italy; **Maria Jose Pueyo**, EOI Zaragoza, Spain; **Bruce Ratcliff**, Academia Caledonian, Spain; **Jolanta Rawska**, School of English "Super Grade," Poland; **Mar Rey**, EOI Del Prat, Spain; **Silke Riegler**, HAW Landshut, Germany; **Pauline Rios**, Rivers, Spain; **Laura Rivero**, EOI La Laguna, Spain; **Carmen Rizo**, EOI Torrevieja, Spain; **Antonio F. Rocha Canizares**, EOI Talavera de la Reina, Spain; **Eva Rodellas Fontiguell**, London English School; **Sara Rojo**, EOI Elche, Spain; **Elena Romea**, UNED, Spain; **Ann Ross**, Centro Linguistico di Ateneo, Italy; **Tyler Ross**, Ingliese for you, Italy; **Susan Royo**, EOI Utebo, Spain; **Asuncion Ruiz Astruga**, EOI Maria Molinar, Spain; **Tamara Ruiz Fernandez**, English Today, Spain; **Soledat Sabate**, FIAC, Spain; **Maria Justa Saenz de Tejad**, ECI Idiomas Bailen, Spain; **Sophia Salaman**, University of Florence, Centro Linguistico de ATENEO, Italy; **Elizabeth Schiller**, Schillers Sprachstudio, Germany; **Carmen Serrano Tierz**, CULM, Spain; **Elizabeth R. Sherman**, Lexis Language Centre, Italy; **Rocio Sierra**, EOI Maspalomas, Spain; **David Silles McLaney**, EOI Majadahonda, Spain; **Alison Slade**, British School Florence, Italy; **Rachael Smith**, Accademia Britannica Toscana, Italy; **Michael Smith**, The Cultural English Centre, Spain; **Sonia Sood**, Oxford School Treviso, Italy; **Monika Stawska**, SJO Pigmalion, Poland; **Izabela Stępniewska**, ZS nr 69, Warszawa / British School Otwock, Poland; **Rocío Stevenson**, R & B Academia, Spain; **Petra Stolinova**, Magic English s.r.o., Czech Republic; **Hana Szulczewska**, UNO (Studium Języków Obcych), Poland; **Tim T.**, STP, Spain; **Vera Tauchmanova**, Univerzita Hradec Kralove, Czech Republic; **Nina Terry**, Nina School of English, Spain; **Francesca R. Thompson**, British School of East, Italy; **Pilar Tizzard**, Docklands Idiomes, Spain; **Jessica Toro**, International House Zaragoza, Spain; **Christine Tracey**, Università Roma Tre, Italy; **Loredana Trocchi**, L'Aquila, Italy; **Richard Twiggl**, International House Milan, Italy; **Natàlia Verdalet**, EOI Figueres, Spain; **Sergio Viñals**, EOI San Javier, Spain; **Edith von Sundahl-Hiller**, Supernova Idiomes, Spain; **Vanda Vyslouzilova**, Academia, Czech Republic; **Helen Waldron**, ELC, Germany; **Leslie Wallace**, Academia Language School, Switzerland; **Monika Wąsowska-Polak**, Akademia Obrony Narodowej, Poland; **Melissa Weaver**, TLC-IH, Switzerland; **Maria Watton**, Centro Lingue Estere CC, Italy; **Dr. Otto Weihs**, IMC FH Krems, Austria; **Kate Williams**, Oxford House Barcelona, Spain; **June Winterflood**, Academia Language School, Switzerland; **Ailsa Wood**, Cooperativa Babel, Italy; **Irene Zamora**, www.speakwithirene.com, Spain; **Coro Zapata**, EOIP Pamplona, Spain; **Gloria Zaragoza**, Alicante University, Spain; **Cristina Zêzere**, EOI Torrelavega, Spain

LATIN AMERICA **Fernando Arcos**, Santo Tomás University, Chile; **Ricardo Barreto**, Bridge School, Brazil; **Beth Bartlett**, Centro Cultural Colombo Americano, Cali, Colombia; **Julie Patricia Benito Lugo**, Universidad Central, Colombia; **Ana Luisa Bley Soriano**, Universidad UCINF, Chile; **Gabriela Brun**, I.S.F.D N 129, Argentina; **Talita Burlamaqui**, UFAM, Brazil; **Lourdes Leonides Canta Lozano**, Fac. De Ciencias Biolgicas UANL, Mexico; **Claudia Castro**, Stratford Institute – Moreno-Bs.As, Argentina; **Fabrício Cruz**, Britanic, Brazil; **Lisa Davies**, British Council, Colombia; **Adriana de Blasis**, English Studio Ciudad de Mercedes, Argentina; **Nora Abraira de Lombardo**, Cultural Inglesa de Mercedes, Argentina; **Bronwyn Donohue**, British Council, Colombia; **Andrea C. Duran**, Universidad Externado de Colombia; **Phil Elias**, British Council, Colombia; **Silvia C. Enríquez**, Esculea de Lenguas. Universidad Nacional de La Plata, Argentina; **Freddy Espinoza**, Universidad UCINF, Chile; **Maria de Lourdes Fernandes Silva**, The First Steps School, Brazil; **Doris Flores**, Santo Tomás English Program, Chile; **Hilda Flor-Páez**, Universidad Catolica Santiago de Guayaquil, Ecuador; **Lauriston Freitas**, Cooplem Idiomas, Brazil; **Alma Delia Frias Puente**, UANL, Mexico; **Sandra Gacitua Matus**, Universidad de la Frontera, Chile; **Gloria Garcia**, IPI Ushuaia-Tierra del Fuego, Argentina; **Alma Delia Garcia Ensastegui**, UAEM, Mexico; **Karina Garcia Gonzalez**, Universidad Panamericana, Mexico; **Miguel García Rojas**, UNMSM, Peru; **Macarena González Mena**, Universidad Tecnológica de Chile, Inacap, Chile; **Diana Granado**, Advanced English, Colombia; **Paul Christopher Graves**, Universidad Mayor, Chile; **Mabel Gutierrez**, British Council, Colombia; **Niamh Harnett**, Universidad Externado de Colombia, Colombia; **Elsa Hernandez**, English Time Institute, Argentina; **Reinaldo Hernández Sordo**, DUOC UC, Chile; **Eduardo Icaza**, CEN, Ecuador; **Kenel Joseph**, Haitian-American Institute, Haiti; **Joel Kellogg**, British Council, Colombia; **Sherif Ebrahim Khakil**, Chapingo Universidad Autonoma Chapingo, Mexico; **Cynthia Marquez**, Instituto Guatemalteco Americano, Guatemala; **Aaron McCarroll**, Universidad Sergio Arboleda, Colombia; **Milagro Machado**, SISE Institute, Peru; **Marta de Faria e Cunha Monteiro**, Federal University of Amazonas – UFAM, Brazil; **Lucía Murillo Sardi**, Instituto Británico, Peru; **Ricardo A. Nausa**, Universidad de los Andes, Colombia; **Andrea Olmos Bernal**, Universidad de Guadalajara, Mexico; **M. Edu Lizzete Olvera Dominguez**, Universidad Autonoma de Baja California Sur, Mexico; **Blanca Ortecho**,

Universidad Cesar Vallejo Centro de Idiomas, Peru; **Jim Osorio**, Instituto Guatemalteco Americano, Guatemala; **Erika del Carmen Partida Velasco**, Univam, Mexico; **Mrs. Katterine Pavez**, Universidad de Atacama, Chile; **Sergio Peña**, Universidad de La Frontera, Chile; **Leonor Cristina Peñafort Camacho**, Universidad Autónoma de Occidente, Colombia; **Tom Rickman**, British Council, Colombia; **Olga Lucia Rivera**, Universidad Externado de Colombia, Colombia; **Maria-Eugenia Ruiz Brand**, DUOC UC, Chile; **Gabriela S. Eguiarte**, London School, Mexico; **Majid Safadaran**, Instituto Cultural Peruano Norteamericano, Peru; **María Ines Salinas**, UCASAL, Argentina; **Ruth Salomon-Barkmeyer**, UNILINGUAS – UNISINOS, Brazil; **Mario Castillo Sanchez Hidalgo**, Universidad Panamericana, Mexico; **Katrina J. Schmidt**, Universidad de Los Andes, Colombia; **Jacqueline Sedore**, The Language Company, Chile; **Lourdes Angelica Serrano Herrera**, Adler Schule, Mexico; **Antonio Diego Sousa de Oliveira**, Federal University of Amazonas, Brazil; **Padraig Sweeney**, Universidad Sergio Arboleda, Colombia; **Edith Urquiza Parra**, Centro Universitario México, Mexico; **Eduardo Vásquez**, Instituto Chileno Britanico de Cultura, Chile; **Patricia Villasante**, Idiomas Católica, Peru; **Malaika Wilson**, The Language Company, Chile; **Alejandra Zegpi-Pons**, Universidad Católica de Temuco, Chile; **Boris Zevallos**, Universidad Cesar Vallejo Centro de Idiomas, Peru; **Wilma Zurita Beltran**, Universidad Central del Ecuador, Ecuador

THE MIDDLE EAST Chaker Ali Mhamdi, Buraimi University College, Oman; **Salama Kamal Shohayb**, Al-Faisal International Academy, Saudi Arabia

TURKEY M. Mine Bağ, Sabanci University, School of Languages; **Suzanne Campion**, Istanbul University; **Daniel Chavez**, Istanbul University Language Center; **Asuman Cincioğlu**, Istanbul University; **Hatice Çelikkanat**, Istanbul Esenyurt University; **Güneş Yurdasiper Dal**, Maltepe University; **Angeliki Douri**, Istanbul University Language Center; **Zia Foley**, Istanbul University; **Frank Foroutan**, Istanbul University Language Center; **Nicola Frampton**, Istanbul University; **Merve Güler**, Istanbul University; **H. Ibrahim Karabulut**, Dumlupınar University; **Catherine McKimm**, Istanbul University; **Merve Oflaz**, Dogus University; **Burcu Özgül**, Istanbul University; **Yusuf Özmenekşe**, Istanbul University Language Center; **Lanlo Pinter**, Istanbul University Language Center; **Ahmet Rasim**, Amasya University; **Diana Maria Rios Hoyos**, Istanbul University Language Center; **Jose Rodrigues**, Istanbul University; **Dilek Eryılmaz Salkı**, Ozyegin University; **Merve Selcuk**, Istanbul Kemerburgaz University; **Mehdi Solhi Andarab**, Istanbul Medipol University; **Jennifer Stephens**, Istanbul University; **Özgür Şahan**, Bursa Technical University; **Fatih Yücel**, Beykent University

UNITED KINGDOM Sarah Ali, Nottingham Trent International College, Nottingham; **Rolf Donald**, Eastbourne School of English, Eastbourne, East Sussex; **Nadine Early**, ATC Language Schools, Dublin, Ireland; **Dr. Sarah Ekdawi**, Oxford School of English, Oxford; **Glynis Ferrer**, LAL Torbay, Paignton Devon; **Diarmuid Fogarty**,

INTO Manchester, Manchester; **Ryan Hannan**, Hampstead School of English, London; **Neil Harris**, ELTS, Swansea University, Swansea; **Claire Hunter**, Edinburgh School of English, Edinburgh, Scotland; **Becky Ilk**, LAL Torbay, Paignton; **Kirsty Matthews**, Ealing, Hammersmith & West London's college, London; **Amanda Mollaghan**, British Study Centres London, London; **Shila Nadar**, Twin ECL, London; **Sue Owens**, Cambridge Academy of English, Girton, Cambridge; **Caroline Preston**, International House Newcastle, Newcastle upon Tyne; **Ruby Rennie**, University of Edinburgh, Edinburgh, Scotland; **Howard Smith**, Oxford House College, London; **Yijie Wang**, The University of Edinburgh, Scotland; **Alex Warren**, Eurotraining, Bournemouth

UNITED STATES Christina H. Appel, ELS Educational Services, Manhattan, NY; **Nicole Bollhalder**, Stafford House, Chicago, IL; **Rachel Bricker**, Arizona State University, Tempe, AZ; **Kristen Brown**, Massachusetts International Academy, Marlborough, MA; **Tracey Brown**, Parkland College, Champaign, IL; **Peter Campisi**, ELS Educational Services, Manhattan, NY; **Teresa Cheung**, North Shore Community College, Lynn, MA; **Tyler Clancy**, ASC English, Boston, MA; **Rachael David**, Talk International, Miami, FL; **Danielle De Koker**, ELS Educational Services, New York, NY; **Diana Djaboury**, Mesa Community College, Mesa, AZ; **Mark Elman**, Talk International, Miami, FL; **Dan Gauran**, EC English, Boston, MA; **Kerry Gilman**, ASC English, Boston, MA; **Heidi Guenther**, ELS Educational Services, Manhattan, NY; **Emily Herrick**, University of Nebraska-Lincoln, Lincoln, NE; **Kristin Homuth**, Language Center International, Southfield, MI; **Alexander Ingle**, ALPS Language School, Seattle, WA; **Eugenio Jimenez**, Lingua Language Center at Broward College, Miami, FL; **Mahalia Joeseph**, Lingua Language Center at Broward College, Miami, FL; **Melissa Kaufman**, ELS Educational Services, Manhattan, NY; **Kristin Kradolfer Espinar**, MILA, Miami, FL; **Larissa Long**, TALK International, Fort Lauderdale, FL; **Mercedes Martinez**, Global Language Institute, Minneapolis, MN; **Ann McCrory**, San Diego Continuing Education, San Diego, CA; **Simon McDonough**, ASC English, Boston, MA; **Dr. June Ohrnberger**, Suffolk County Community College, Brentwood, NY; **Fernanda Ortiz**, Center for English as a Second Language at the University of Arizona, Tuscon, AZ; **Roberto S. Quintans**, Talk International, Miami, FL; **Terri J. Rapoport**, ELS, Princeton, NJ; **Alex Sanchez Silva**, Talk International, Miami, FL; **Cary B. Sands**, Talk International, Miami, FL; **Joseph Santaella Vidal**, EC English, Boston, MA; **Angel Serrano**, Lingua Language Center at Broward College, Miami, FL; **Timothy Alan Shaw**, New England School of English, Boston, MA; **Devinder Singh**, The University of Tulsa, Tulsa, OK; **Daniel Stein**, Lingua Language Center at Broward College, Miami, FL; **Christine R. Stesau**, Lingua Language Center at Broward College, Miami, FL; **David Stock**, ELS Educational Services, Manhattan, NY; **Joshua Stone**, Approach International Student Center, Allston, MA; **Maria-Virginia Tanash**, EC English, Boston, MA; **Noraina Vazquez Huyke**, Talk International, Miami, FL

Overview

A REAL-WORLD VIEWPOINT

Whatever your goals and aspirations, *Wide Angle* helps you use English to connect with the world around you. It empowers you to join any conversation and say the right thing at the right time, with confidence.

4 Life

UNIT SNAPSHOT

Who wrote the book *Little Women*? 41
What makes people happy? 44
What is it like to be an actor? 50

What are the people doing?
Is your morning like this?
What do you do every day?

BEHIND THE PHOTO

REAL-WORLD GOAL

Ask someone for the time

1   How many hours a week do you do these things?

Work or study: _____
Do chores: _____
Cook and eat: _____
Have fun: _____
Sleep: _____
Total: _____ / 168 hours

2   Talk with a partner about how many hours a week you do these things.

Start thinking about the topic with relevant, interesting **introduction questions**.

blink

Be inspired by the **vibrant unit opener images** from Blink photography. The international, award-winning photographers bring stories from around the world to life on the page.

Watch the **"Behind the Photo"** video from the photographer.

Apply learning to your own needs with **Real-World Goals**, instantly seeing the benefit of the English you are learning.

"These people are on a bus from New York City to Washington, D.C. It is early in the morning."
Edu Bayer

Enjoy learning with the huge variety of **up-to-date, inventive, and engaging audio and video**.

4.4 Time to Go!

Understand what to say and how to say it with **English For Real**.

These lessons equip you to choose and adapt appropriate language to communicate effectively in any situation.

1 **ACTIVATE** Write the times in numbers.

1	_10:00_	It's ten.	6	_____	It's two oh five.
2	_____	It's eight o'clock.	7	_____	It's one thirty.
3	_____	It's five forty-five.	8	_____	It's ten after four.
4	_____	It's five to ten.	9	_____	It's half past three.
5	_____	It's quarter to eleven.	10	_____	It's quarter past eleven.

2 **USE** Look at the pictures. Say the time in words.

four fifteen (quarter past four)

1
2
3
4
5
6

3  **IDENTIFY** Watch the video. Answer the questions.

1 Max and Andy don't know what time it is because ____
  a they don't have a clock.
  b the power is out.
2 Max gets _____ from his bedroom to see t
  a a watch
  b his phone
3 Max and Andy leave their apartment at _____
  a 10:10
  b 10:30
4 In class, Kevin asks: _____
  a What time is it?
  b Does anybody have the time?
5 Max tells Kevin that the time is _____.
  a 10:45
  b 11:00

REAL-WORLD ENGLISH Asking for the time

When you ask a stranger for the time, you need to get the pe
a polite question.
Excuse me, do you have the time?
Excuse me! Do you know what time it is?

When asking a friend, you can be more direct.
Hey, what time is it?
What's the time?

4 ▶ **ANALYZE** Watch the video again. Write down all th
for the time. Who says them? Compare your answers wi

5 **PREPARE** Work with a partner. Follow the instructions.

■ Choose a situation: friends or strangers.
■ Choose a time.
■ Write a dialogue about asking for the time. Practice your dialogue.

6 **INTERACT** Work with another pair. Act out your dialogues for each other.
Were they friends or strangers?

ENGLISH FOR REAL

48

GO ONLINE
to create your own version
of the English For Real video.

49

Step into the course with **English For Real videos** that mimic real-life interactions. You can record your voice and respond in real time for out-of-class practice that is relevant to your life.

COMPREHENSIVE SYLLABUS

Ensure progress in all skills with a pedagogically consistent and appropriately leveled syllabus.

1 ACTIVATE How are the people related? Make sentences using the words.

| mother | father | husband | wife | son | daughter | brother | sister |

🔖 Oxford 3000™

She's his wife. He's their son.

▼ VOCABULARY

The 🔖 Oxford 3000™ is a word list containing the most important words to learn in English. The words are chosen based on frequency in the Oxford English Corpus and relevance to learners of English. Every word is aligned to the CEFR, guiding you on the words you should know at each level.

2 WHAT'S YOUR ANGLE? Think about a family you know (from TV, a book, or real life). Who is your favorite family member? Why?

The Simpsons are a famous family from TV. My favorite family member is the daughter, Lisa, because she's a good person and she's smart. She's not bad like her brother Bart!

GRAMMAR IN CONTEXT Simple present

We use the simple present to talk about habits and routines.
*I **work** in the morning. I **go** to school in the evening.*

We also use the simple present to talk about facts and opinions.
*The Marches **live** in Concord, Massachusetts. They **love** it there.*

We add *-s* to verbs with *he / she / it*. If the verb ends in *-o, -s, -x, -z, -ch,* or *-sh*, we add *-es*.
*Mr. March **works** for the army. His job **finishes** at 2 a.m.*

The verb *have* is irregular.
*They **have** four daughters.*
*She **has blond** hair.*

See Grammar focus on page 162.

▼ GRAMMAR

The carefully graded grammar syllabus ensures you encounter the most relevant language at the right point in your learning.

3 IDENTIFY Read the description of a family from literature. Find the verbs.

 ## The Marches

Little Women (1868) by Louisa May Alcott tells the story of the March family. The family in the book is similar to the author's life and family. The main character, Jo, is similar to Louisa.

Mrs. March is a busy, happy, kind woman. Her husband, Mr. March, works for the army and is away in the Civil War. She misses her husband, but she isn't lonely. They have four daughters: Jo, Meg, Beth, and Amy. Jo is 15 years old and intelligent. She writes a lot of stories. She wants to be an author. Her sister Meg is 16 and pretty. She wants to have a rich, important husband. Beth is 13. She loves music and wants to be a musician, but she is not strong. She is often sick, too. Amy is 12. She has blond hair and is beautiful.

The family spends a lot of time together. They also spend a lot of time with their neighbors, the Laurence family.

—Adapted from *The Oxford Companion to American Literature* (6 ed.) by James D. Hart and Phillip W. Leininger

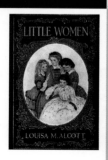

Oxford Reference is a trusted source of over two million authentic academic texts.

Free access to the Oxford Reference site is included with Student Books 4, 5, and 6.

4.3 Be Successful!

1 ACTIVATE Work with a partner. Which things does a successful person do? Add a ✓ or ✗ to the activities.

1 go to work late ☐
2 spend time with family ☐
3 have a lot of free time ☐
4 watch a lot of TV ☐

5 go to bed late at night ☐
6 work on weekends ☐
7 play games at work ☐
8 get up early in the morning ☐

GRAMMAR IN CONTEXT Simple present: Negative forms

We form the simple present negative with subject + *don't / doesn't* + verb.

Use *don't* with *I, you, we,* and *they*:
*I **don't** work on Sundays.*
Use *doesn't* with *he, she,* and *it*:
*He **doesn't** watch TV.*
*It **doesn't** help you.*

See Grammar focus on page 162.

2 INTEGRATE Look at the list from Exercise 1. Make sentences about what successful people do and don't do.

A successful person doesn't go to work late. A successful person spends time with her family.

3 IDENTIFY Look at the poster. What is it for?

LISTENING SKILL Contractions (short forms) with *be* **and simple present negatives**

Negative short forms can be hard to hear when people speak quickly. With the verb *be*, you need to listen for *be* + *not*. With other simple present negative verbs, you need to listen for *doesn't* or *don't* and the main verb.
*I'm **not** tired.*
*Chris **isn't** a good worker. He's **not** successful.*
*He **doesn't** go to work early.*
*They **don't** do their homework.*

4 IDENTIFY Before you listen to Ray Rich, practice understanding simple present positive and negative forms. Listen to the sentences and choose the form of the verb you hear.

1 positive / negative
2 positive / negative
3 positive / negative
4 positive / negative
5 positive / negative

Ray Rich
Do's and Don'ts for Successful People
Tuesday, November 5
7:00 p.m.
Shea Hall

46

5 ASSESS Listen to the talk and choose the correct endings to the sentence.
In Ray Rich's opinion, a successful person…

a has a lot of money.
b has a big house.

c has a lot of good friends.
d has an interesting job.

6 INTEGRATE Listen again. What does Ray say? Choose the correct answers.

1 It's hard / It's not hard to be successful.
2 He cleans / doesn't clean his desk every day.
3 He works / doesn't work on Saturdays.
4 He works / doesn't work on Sundays.
5 He talks / doesn't talk to his friends at the office.

6 He uses / doesn't use the Internet at the office.
7 His friends are / aren't successful people.
8 He watches / doesn't watch TV.
9 TV is / isn't good.

7 WHAT'S YOUR ANGLE? In your opinion, does Ray give good advice? Why or why not?

VOCABULARY DEVELOPMENT Prepositions of time *on, in,* **and** *at*

Use *in* with times of the day.
in the morning   in the afternoon   in the evening
Use *at* for specific times and with *night*.
at 9 a.m.   at night
Use *on* for days.
on Monday   on weekends   on New Year's Day   on Saturday mornings
The days of the week are:

Monday	Tuesday	Wednesday	Thursday	Friday	Saturday	Sunday
					weekend	

8 BUILD Listen and repeat the days of the week. What's your favorite day of the week? What's your favorite time of day? Tell a partner.

9 USE Complete the sentences with *in, on,* and *at*. Then make the sentences true for you.

1 He sleeps late _____ weekends.
2 I do housework _____ 2:00 _____ the afternoon.
3 She goes to work _____ 10:00 _____ the morning.
4 We see our friends _____ night.
5 My English class is _____ Mondays, Wednesdays, and Fridays.

10 INTERACT Work with a partner. Make a list of three things a successful student does and three things he / she doesn't do. Share with the class.

47

◤ READING AND LISTENING

Explicit reading and listening skills focus on helping you access and assimilate information confidently in this age of rapid information.

Build confidence with the **activation-presentation-practice-production** method, with activities moving from controlled to less controlled, with an increasing level of challenge.

8 INTERACT Tell a partner about your family. Make sure you use the correct simple present endings.

WRITING SKILL Using *also* **and** *too*

We use *also* and *too* to add information. Notice where the words are in the sentences.
*My sister likes books. She **also** likes music.*
*I'm from Mexico. My wife is **also** from Mexico.*
*My parents live in Laos. My brother and his family live there, **too**.*

9 PREPARE Rewrite the second sentence. Use *also* or *too*.

1 You have three children? I have three children.
   (too) _____ I have three children, too. _____
2 I have two sisters. I have a brother.
   (too) _____
3 We have a cat. Our neighbors have a cat.
   (also) _____

◤ WRITING

The writing syllabus focuses on the writing styles needed for today, using a **process writing approach** of **prepare-plan-draft-review-correct** to produce the best possible writing.

PRONUNCIATION SKILL /s/, /z/, /ɪz/ in simple present verbs

We pronounce the *-s* or *-es* differently depending on the sound that comes before it. Listen for the three different endings.
wants
loves
misses
Words that end with /s/, /z/, /ʃ/, /tʃ/, and /dʒ/ have an extra syllable when *-s* or *-es* is added.

5 NOTICE How many syllables does each word have? Write *1* or *2*. Then listen and check.

1 like _____ likes _____
2 go _____ goes _____
3 choose _____ chooses _____

4 teach _____ teaches _____
5 wash _____ washes _____
6 play _____ plays _____

6 DEVELOP Listen and repeat.

/s/	works	gets up	likes	wants	sleeps
/z/	lives	goes	needs	spends	listens

◤ SPEAKING

Speaking and **pronunciation skills** build the functional language you need outside of class.

A BLENDED LEARNING APPROACH

Make the most of *Wide Angle* with opportunities for relevant, personalized learning outside of class.

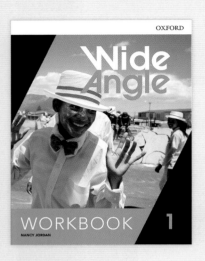

ONLINE PRACTICE

When you see this icon in your Student Book, go online to extend your learning.

With Online Practice you can:

- Review the skills taught in every lesson and get **instant feedback**.
- Practice grammar and vocabulary through **fun games**.
- Access **all audio and video** material. Use the Access Code in the front of this Student Book to log in for the first time at wideangle.oxfordonlinepractice.com.

WORKBOOK

Your Workbook provides additional practice for every unit of the Student Book.

Each unit includes:

- An entirely new reading with skill practice linked to **Oxford Reference**.
- Support for the **Discussion Board**, helping students to master online writing.
- Listening comprehension and skill practice using the **Unit Review Podcast**.
- Real-life English practice linked to the **English For Real** videos.
- **Grammar** and **vocabulary** exercises related to the unit topic.

Use your Workbook for homework or self-study.

FOCUS ON THE TEACHER

The Teacher's Resource Center at wideangle.oxfordonlinepractice.com saves teachers time by integrating and streamlining access to the following support:

- **Teacher's Guide**, including fun **More to Say** pronunciation activities and **professional development** materials.
- **Easy-to-use** learning management system for the student Online Practice, **answer keys**, **audio**, lots of **extra activities**, **videos**, and so much more.

The **Classroom Presentation Tool** brings the Student Book to life for heads-up lessons. Class audio, video, and answer keys, as well as teaching notes, are available online or offline, and are updated across your devices.

1 Self

Describe the image.

How is she the same as you?

How is she different from you?

BEHIND THE PHOTO

1 **Match. Then compare your answers with a partner.**

1	A country	a	Europe
2	A number	b	French
3	A capital city	c	Japan
4	A language	d	100
5	A continent	e	Ankara

2 **What are your country and language?**

REAL-WORLD GOAL

Introduce yourself to some new people at your language school!

1.1 We're Famous For...

1 ACTIVATE Match the countries to the items.

the United Kingdom	Argentina	Spain	Egypt	Brazil
the United States	Japan	Mexico	South Korea	Germany

1 _____

6 _____

2 _____

7 _____

3 _____

8 _____

4 _____

9 _____

5 _____

10 _____

GRAMMAR IN CONTEXT The verb *be*: Positive and subject pronouns

Be is an irregular verb. It has three forms in the simple present tense: *am*, *is*, and *are*.
The subject pronouns are: *I, you, we, they, he, she*, and *it*.

I am / I'm Susana.

We / You / They are students. *We're / You're / They're in Asia.*

He / She / It is Spanish. *He's / She's / It's from Spain.*

See Grammar focus on page 159.

2 IDENTIFY Choose the correct form of *be*.

1 Germany *am / is / are* in Europe.
2 You *am / is / are* in class.
3 I *am / is / are* a student.
4 Argentina and Brazil *am / is / are* in South America.
5 My friend and I *am / is / are* teachers.
6 Mr. Kato *am / is / are* from Japan.
7 Mariana *am / is / are* from Argentina.

3 APPLY Rewrite the sentences from Exercise 2 using a pronoun and the short form of *be*.

It's in Europe.

4 WHAT'S YOUR ANGLE? Where are you from? What is your country famous for?
Write sentences.

I'm from Brazil. We're famous for soccer, samba music, and coffee.

Spotlight on International Students

Meet some of our new students from around the world!

Mariana Bianchi

I'm a student and musician from Buenos Aires. It's the capital city of Argentina. Our official language is Spanish. The name of our country means "the land of silver" in Spanish. But the Argentinean currency is not silver. It's the peso!

Hanna and Emilia Fischer

We're from Germany. It's a beautiful country! Our language is German, and our currency is the euro. The German capital is Berlin, but we're from Munich in the south. I'm a businesswoman, and my sister is a server in a restaurant.

Kaito Fuchida

I'm from Tokyo, the capital city of Japan. I'm a student there. Japanese is the official language of Japan. My father is Japanese, but my mother is Korean. They're both scientists. Our currency is the yen.

Karim Abadi

My name is Karim. I'm from the city of Alexandria in Egypt. I'm a French teacher here. Alexandria isn't the capital city. It's Cairo. Our currency is the Egyptian pound.

—Adapted from *A Guide to Countries of the World* (4th ed.) by Christopher Riches and Peter Stalker

5 **INTEGRATE** Read about the students and their countries.

 READING SKILL Recognizing nouns and pronouns

After a noun, we can use a pronoun. This avoids repetition. Look for the noun to understand the pronoun.

Kaito is a student. He is from Japan.

6 **IDENTIFY** Read the Reading skill. Find one noun and its pronoun in each student profile.

I'm a student and musician from <u>Buenos Aires</u>. (It's) the capital city of Argentina.

7 **APPLY** Read the student profiles again. Complete the table.

Student's name	Job	Country	Student's city	Capital city	Currency
Mariana	musician, student				

8 **WHAT'S YOUR ANGLE?** Fill in the last row of the table in Exercise 7 with your information. Share with the class.

 VOCABULARY DEVELOPMENT Nationalities

Most nationalities are formed by adding an ending to the name of a country or part of a country's name. The most common endings are *-n / -an / -ian*, *-ish*, and *-ese*.

Mexico → Mexican	*Brazil → Brazilian*
Poland → Polish	*China → Chinese*

Some nationalities are irregular. For example:

Peru → Peruvian   *France → French*   *Spain → Spanish*
the United Kingdom → British   *the United States → American*

9 **BUILD** Complete the chart with the nationality for each country.

-n	-an	-ian	-ish	-ese
Korea:	Chile:	Italy:	Sweden:	Vietnam:
Russia:	Mexico: Mexican	Canada:	Turkey:	Japan:

10 **WHAT'S YOUR ANGLE?** Add other countries to the chart in Exercise 9. What do you know about each country? Write the name of one person or one thing from each country. Include your country.

Mexico is a country in North America. Gael García Bernal is Mexican. Tacos are an example of Mexican food.

1.2 I'm a Rising Star!

1 ACTIVATE Complete the form.

United States   (801) 976-2105   18   David   d.rod.123@bmail.com   Asheville   12/15/99

Rising Stars Career College

First name: _____

Last name: _Rodrigues_____

Phone number: _____

Email: _____

Address: _12 Pleasant Street_____

City: _____

State: _North Carolina_____

Country: _____

Date of birth: _____

Age: _____

Career I want to train for:

☐ musician   ☐ TV chef

☐ driver   ☐ teacher

☐ actor / actress   ☐ professional athlete

☐ artist

☐ other

Apply now! Classes start 9/1!

GRAMMAR IN CONTEXT Questions with _be_

We form _yes/no questions_ with:
Am / Are / Is + subject?

We form short answers with:
Yes + subject + _am / are / is._
_No_ + subject + _'m not / aren't / isn't._

Is he _a chef?_   _Yes,_ **he is**.
Are you _a student here?_   _No,_ **I'm not**.

We can form _wh-_ questions with _be_:
Question word + _am / are / is_ + subject?

We use different question words to ask about different types of information.

What's _your last name?_   **Where** _are you from?_
When _is the class?_   **How** _old are you?_

See Grammar focus on page 159.

2 🔊 **IDENTIFY** Read the conversation. Complete the questions. Then listen and check.

Amanda: Rising Stars Career College, this is Amanda. Can I help you?

David: Yes, I'd like to apply for some classes.

Amanda: OK. ¹_____ you a student here?

David: No, I'm not.

Amanda: OK. What's your name?

David: My first name is David, and my last name is Rodrigues.

Amanda: Thank you. ²_____ is your phone number?

David: It's (801) 976-2105.

Amanda: ³_____ your email address?

David: It's d.rod.123@bmail.com.

Amanda: OK. ⁴_____ your address?

David: It's 12 Pleasant Street.

Amanda: And ⁵_____ are you from?

David: Asheville, North Carolina.

Amanda: Great. ⁶_____ your date of birth?

David: It's 12/15/99.

Amanda: So ⁷_____ old are you now?

David: I'm 18.

Amanda: And what's your career choice?

David: I want to be a famous chef on TV.

Amanda: You will be, David! You're a rising star!

David: I hope so! ⁸_____ is the first class?

Amanda: It's on 9/1.

David: Thanks!

3 🔊 **INTEGRATE** Listen again. Check your answers from Exercise 1.

4 **INTERACT** Write three questions for a partner. Ask your partner the questions. Switch roles.

A: Where are you from?
B: I'm from Poland.

5 🔊 **VOCABULARY** Complete the chart with the missing numbers. Then listen and repeat.

one	seven	twelve	twenty	six	eleven	five	eighteen	2	19
seventeen	nine	fourteen	fifteen	three	13	16	10	4	8

1	_____	6	_____	11	_____	____	sixteen
____	two	7	_____	12	_____	17	_____
3	_____	____	eight	____	thirteen	18	_____
____	four	9	_____	14	_____	____	nineteen
5	_____	____	ten	15	_____	20	_____

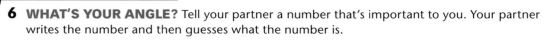

6 **WHAT'S YOUR ANGLE?** Tell your partner a number that's important to you. Your partner writes the number and then guesses what the number is.

Student A: 5, 15, 95

Student B: 5, 15, 95. Is it your date of birth?

Student A: Yes! It is.

A proper noun is the name of a specific person, place, or business (*Ann Jones*, *Paris*, *Village Bank*). Make sure you use capital letters for all proper nouns. Do not use capital letters for common nouns or pronouns except *I*.

7 **IDENTIFY** Find the errors. Rewrite the sentences correctly. If the sentence is correct, write *OK*.

1 His Name is Rasheed._____

2 My Teacher is Ms. collins._____

3 My Friend is from athens._____

4 What countries are the students from?_____

5 My doctor is dr. patel._____

6 Are You from south korea?_____

8 **WRITE** Complete the form with your own information.

Rising Stars Career College

First name: _____

Last name: _____

**Apply now!
Classes start
9/1!**

Phone number: _____

Email: _____

Address: _____

City: _____

State: _____

Country: _____

Date of birth: _____

Age: _____

Career I want to train for:

☐ musician   ☐ teacher

☐ driver   ☐ professional athlete

☐ actor / actress   ☐ other

☐ artist

☐ TV chef

A young chef at a restaurant in Rome, Italy

9 **IMPROVE** Read your form and correct any mistakes.

Check for:

■ correct spelling

■ capitalization of proper nouns

■ correct numbers from 1–20

10 **SHARE** Swap forms with another student. Ask questions with *be* to check their answers.

A: Is your last name Allani?

B: Yes, it is.

A: Are you 22 years old?

B: Yes, I am.

11 **WHAT'S YOUR ANGLE?** Find a form online for something that interests you, like a job, a hotel reservation, a school, or something different. Fill it out and share it with the class.

1.3 Who's Who?

1 ACTIVATE Match the jobs to the images.

a businessman / businesswoman	a doctor	a scientist	a race car driver
an actor / actress	a soccer player	a teacher	an artist
an author	a musician		

 Oxford 3000™

JOB SEARCH

Latest employers | **Articles** | Search by map | Latest resources

10 Best Jobs of This Year

A good job means interesting work or a great salary—or both!

1 $150,000–$315,000
2 $50,000–$8,000,000
3 $35,000–$75,000
4 $50,000–$65,000
5 $60,000–$90,000

6 $30,000–$85,000
7 $1,000,000–$20,000,000
8 $55,000–$85,000
9 $28,000–$150,000
10 $40,000–$50,000

2 WHAT'S YOUR ANGLE? What other jobs do people have? What is your job?

My friend is a nurse. My brother is a police officer. I'm a server at a restaurant.

 LISTENING SKILL Understanding content words in speech

Content words are words that have important meaning in a sentence. Content words are said more clearly and have more stress on them than other words. Words like *the, a, in, and,* and *from* are less important. They are not stressed.

3 APPLY Listen to the quiz. Choose the content words you hear for each person.

a	he	(she)	(author)	(books)	with	and
b	actress	actor	an	and	Kenyan	Mexican
c	he	she	or	scientist	from	United Kingdom
d	she	he	woman	driver	from	United States
e	soccer	in	from	he	she	Uruguay
f	baseball	soccer	he	she	for	Japanese
g	a	artist	actress	Japanese	and	very
h	businessman	businesswoman	from	the	of	Facebook

4 🔊 **INTEGRATE** Listen again. Match each clue to the correct person.

1 **Yayoi Kusama**

2 **Ichiro Suzuki**

3 **Brian Cox**

4 **Mark Zuckerberg**

5 **J.K. Rowling**

6 **Lupita Nyong'o**

7 **Danica Patrick**

8 **Luis Suárez**

5 **WHAT'S YOUR ANGLE?** Who are some famous artists, businesspeople, scientists, sports players, and others from your country? Talk to a partner.

Rafael Nadal is a tennis player from Spain.

> **GRAMMAR IN CONTEXT** *Be*: Negative
>
> We use *not* to make *be* negative. We use *be* + *not* to say that something is not true.
> *He is **not** an actor or a sports player. He's a scientist and an author.*
> We use short forms in spoken English.
> *She **isn't** from the United States.*

See Grammar focus on page 159.

6 **IDENTIFY** Choose the correct word.

1 J.K. Rowling *isn't / aren't* a musician.
2 Lupita Nyong'o and Brian Cox *isn't / aren't* from the United States.
3 Ichiro Suzuki and Yayoi Kusama *is / are* from Japan.
4 Danica Patrick *isn't / aren't* a man.
5 J.K. Rowling *is / are* British.
6 Mark Zuckerberg and Luis Suárez *is / are* men.

7 **USE** Write the correct positive or negative form of *be* to complete the sentences about the people from the quiz.

1 Mark Zuckerberg_____American. He_____Spanish.
2 Danica Patrick_____a soccer player. She_____a race car driver.
3 J.K. Rowling and Brian Cox _____from the United Kingdom. They _____actors.
4 Yayoi Kusama_____Korean. She _____Japanese. Her art _____interesting and popular.
5 Luis Suárez and Ichiro Suzuki_____both sports players. Suárez_____ a soccer player. Suzuki_____a soccer player.
6 Lupita Nyong'o and Yayoi Kusama_____both famous women. They _____authors.

8 **WHAT'S YOUR ANGLE?** What's your dream job? Ask your classmates the question. Make a list of dream jobs for your class. How many people share your dream?

1.4 Nice to Meet You!

1 **ACTIVATE** Look at the pictures. Where are they? What is their relationship? Why do you think so? Talk with a partner.

2 ▶ **IDENTIFY** Watch the video. Read the expressions and check all the possible boxes. Discuss your ideas with the class.

	Greeting	Introduction	Friends/classmates	Teacher/student
1 "Hello."	☐	☐	☐	☐
2 "Hey!"	☐	☐	☐	☐
3 "I'm Max."	☐	☐	☐	☐
4 "Nice to meet you."	☐	☐	☐	☐
5 "Hey, what's up?"	☐	☐	☐	☐
6 "Hey, how are you doing?"	☐	☐	☐	☐
7 "Good morning."	☐	☐	☐	☐
8 "My name is Karen Lopez."	☐	☐	☐	☐

REAL-WORLD ENGLISH Greetings and introductions

We use different ways of greeting people in different situations. When we talk to friends, family, or classmates, we feel relaxed. We might say *Hi* or *Hey!*, *What's up?*, *How's it going?*, or *How are you doing?*

If we talk to an older person, someone we don't know well, or our boss or teacher, we are less relaxed. We say *Hello* or *Good morning / afternoon*, and *How are you?*

When we meet people for the first time, we use introductions: *I'm…*, *My name is…*, and *Nice to meet you.*

3 ▶ **ANALYZE** Watch the video again. Discuss the questions.

1 How does Max greet Andy? Why?
2 Are Andy and Kevin strangers or friends? How can you tell?
3 Is Kevin's greeting to Karen Lopez correct or not correct? Why?

4 ASSESS Look at the photos. Answer the questions.

1 Where are the people?
2 What is their relationship? Why do you think so?
3 What do you think they are saying?

5 INTEGRATE Work with a partner. Choose two images from Exercise 4. Write the conversations. Use at least four expressions from the box in each conversation.

Hello.	Hi!	Good morning/afternoon/evening.
Hey!	How are you?	How's it going?
Fine, how are you?	Great, and you?	Good, thanks!
My name's…	My name is…	I'm…
Nice to meet you.	Nice to meet you, too.	

6 INTERACT Work with another pair. Act out your conversations.
Can they guess which image each conversation is for?

GO ONLINE
to create your own version
of the English For Real video.

1.5 All About Me

1 ACTIVATE You want to join a gym. What personal information does the gym need from you? Brainstorm a list.

2 **IDENTIFY** Listen to the conversation. Choose the correct answers.

1 The man's name is *Greg* / *Craig*.
2 The man's last name is *Mitchell* / *Michel*.
3 The man is from *Canada* / *the United States*.
4 His address is *116 Portnoy Street* / *16 Portland Street*.
5 His phone number is *(421) 765-2398* / *(401) 769-2358*.

 PRONUNCIATION SKILL Sounds of the alphabet

Practice reading the letters of the alphabet. These will help you spell words and understand when people spell words for you.

A a   B b   C c   D d   E e   F f   G g   H h   I i   J j   K k   L l   M m
N n   O o   P p   Q q   R r   S s   T t   U u   V v   W w   X x   Y y   Z z

---

3 **DEVELOP** Listen and repeat the letters.

4 WHAT'S YOUR ANGLE? Write the names of three people and three places you know. Spell them for a partner while your partner writes. Guess why the people and places are important to your partner. Switch roles.

Student A: W-A-R-S-A-W.
Student B: Are you from Warsaw?
Student A: Yes, I am.

SPEAKING Giving personal information

When you give information about yourself, speak slowly and clearly. Be ready to answer questions and repeat information. Be ready to spell your name and names of places.

---

5 INTEGRATE You work at the gym at an international college. A student needs an ID card. What questions do you ask the student? Use the ID card below to help you.

6 INTERACT Work with a partner. Act out the scenario. Make an ID card. Then switch roles.

Student A: You are calling the gym to order an ID card. You must give the person at the gym all of your information and spell the names.

Student B: You work at the gym. A student calls, but you don't have his or her information in the computer. You must write all the information. Ask him/her questions. All the information must be correct—make sure you ask the student to spell names: *How do you spell that?*

2 Things

What is his job?

What things can you see in the picture?

Describe the things you see.

BEHIND THE PHOTO

1 Which four things do you need in class? Choose the correct answers.

- [ ] a book
- [ ] a car
- [ ] a pen
- [ ] a phone number
- [ ] a teacher
- [ ] a notebook
- [ ] an address
- [ ] a doctor

2 Work with a partner and add more things.

REAL-WORLD GOAL

Order a drink at a coffee shop

1 ACTIVATE Describe the picture. When do you give gifts? What is a good gift for each occasion?

birthday—a box of chocolates

GRAMMAR IN CONTEXT Singular and plural nouns

Most nouns have a singular and plural form.

We use *a / an* with singular nouns. Use *an* for nouns that start with a vowel sound.

a bag   *an* idea
a European country (not an European)

To form most plural nouns, add *-s*.

gift → gifts   *game → games*

Some plural nouns are irregular.

man → men   *woman → women*
child → children   *person → people*

We don't use *a / an* with plural nouns.

Picture frames aren't expensive.

See Grammar focus on page 160.

2 IDENTIFY Find each item in the picture and number it. Then add *a* or *an*.

1 _a_ game _games_____
2 ____ box _____
3 ____ bag _____
4 ____ animal _____
5 ____ child _____
6 ____ picture frame _____

Home | About | Search

Gift Ideas for All Ages

Need a gift for a friend or someone in your family? Here are some ideas to help you.

a picture frame $5–$25

A picture of friends or family in a frame is a very special gift.

a fun game $8–$60

People are happy when they're playing a game!

colored pencils and a coloring book $10–$30

This gift is good for a four-year-old…or a 34-year-old! Coloring is popular now with adults and children. A great idea and not expensive.

concert tickets $15–$100

Music concerts are for everyone, from age one to 101!

a Peruvian bag $12 small/$45 big

These bags are cool and colorful! The big bags are great for students, but everyone can use a Peruvian bag.

a hot air balloon ride $200–$300

It's expensive, but it's an exciting idea!

5 IDENTIFY Find the singular and plural nouns in the article. Complete the chart.

Singular	Plural
gift	ideas

6 WHAT'S YOUR ANGLE? Which gift ideas from the article are good for people you know? Who?

> **READING SKILL Recognizing numbers in a text**
>
> Numbers give you useful information such as ages, prices, dates, and times. Numbers can be words (*one, five, thirteen, twenty,* etc.) or numerals (*1, 5, 13, 20,* etc.).

> **VOCABULARY DEVELOPMENT Numbers 21–101**
>
> | | |
> | --- | --- |
> | 20 *twenty* | 60 *sixty* |
> | 30 *thirty* | 70 *seventy* |
> | 40 *forty* | 80 *eighty* |
> | 50 *fifty* | 90 *ninety* |
>
> 21 = twenty-one
>
> 33 = thirty-three
>
> 99 = ninety-nine
>
> 101 = one hundred and one (or a hundred and one)

7 BUILD Listen and repeat the numbers from the box.

8 DEVELOP Write the numbers in words. Read them aloud.

1 41 _forty-one_
2 52 _____
3 36 _____

4 64 _____
5 87 _____
6 75 _____

9 INTEGRATE Read the article again. Look for the numbers. Which gift…

1 is five to twenty-five dollars?
2 is fifteen to one hundred dollars?
3 is more than one hundred dollars?
4 is eight dollars for a cheap one and sixty for an expensive one?
5 is twelve dollars for a small one and forty-five for a big one?
6 is good for people ages 4 to 34?

10 INTERACT Work with a partner. Add two gift ideas to the article. Include prices and a short description.

2.2 You Need This!

1 VOCABULARY Complete the sentences with the adjectives.

| big | small | ugly | beautiful | new | old | white | black |

🔖 Oxford 3000™

1

This car is _____.

2

This is a(n) _____ car.

3

These cellphones are _____.

4

These are _____ cellphones.

5

This bag is _____.

6

This is a _____ bag.

7

This is a(n) _____ picture.

8

This picture is _____.

2 🔊 USE Write sentences. Then listen and check.

1 this music / old   *This music is old.*

2 my bag / black   _____

3 it / old / school   _____

4 these phones / new   _____

5 your children / beautiful   _____

6 those / ugly / houses   _____

7 that / big / country   _____

3 ASSESS Look at the ad. Discuss the questions.

1 What is the product?
2 What is the number *1878*? Why is it important?
3 What's the name of the company? Whose company is it?

—Adapted from *The Oxford Companion to British History*, 2nd ed., edited by Robert Crowcroft and John Cannon

4 IDENTIFY Find five adjectives in the ad. What people or things do they describe?

exciting (T-Phone)

We use *this* or *these* with nouns to talk about people or things that are near us. They go before the noun. We use *this* with singular nouns and *these* with plural nouns.

This phone is great! ***These*** phones aren't expensive.

We use *that* or *those* with nouns to talk about people or things that aren't very near us. We use *that* with singular nouns and *those* with plural nouns.

That phone is white.
Those phones are black.

This, that, these, and *those* can also be pronouns.

This is Caroline.
Who is ***that?***

See Grammar focus on page 160.

5 **DEVELOP** Put the words in order to make statements.

1 this / good / is / product / a   →   This is a good product.
2 old / this / is / phone   →   _____
3 are / books / those / important   →   _____
4 bag / nice / a / that / is   →   _____
5 car / expensive / is / that   →   _____
6 these / pictures / big / are   →   _____

6 **BUILD** Choose the correct words.

1 (This)/ *These* is my address.
2 *That* / *Those* is a fun game.
3 *This* / *These* computers are expensive.

4 *That* / *Those* houses are very old.
5 *This* / *These* books are interesting.
6 *That* / *Those* music is exciting.

When you aren't sure how to spell something, check your textbook or a dictionary.

~~adress~~ address

7 **IDENTIFY** Find the spelling mistake in each sentence. Write the correct sentence.

1 This is a grate book.   This is a great book.
2 These glasses are wite.   _____
3 This ad is intresting.   _____
4 This is my neu car.   _____
5 These pens are cheep.   _____
6 That's a nise bag.   _____

8 **WRITE** Choose one of the products from Exercise 1. Write an ad for the product. Use adjectives to describe it.

9 **IMPROVE** Read your ad.

Did you…

■ spell all of the words correctly?
■ use *this, that, these,* and *those* correctly?
■ use adjectives to describe the item?

10 **SHARE** Show your ad to your classmates. Vote for your favorite ad. Why is it your favorite?

11 **WHAT'S YOUR ANGLE?** Find an interesting ad. What is it for? What adjectives does it use? Share the ad with the class.

2.3 What's in Your Bag?

1 ACTIVATE Find the items in the picture.

a cell phone	a wallet	a picture of someone	glasses
money	a car key	house keys	a computer

📖 Oxford 3000™

2 WHAT'S YOUR ANGLE? What things are in your bag? How many? Make a list.

GRAMMAR IN CONTEXT Possessive 's and possessive adjectives

We use possessive 's to talk about things or people that belong to a person, place, or thing. We often use possessive 's with names.

Rachel's wallet is big.

We use possessive adjectives with a noun to talk about possessions, family, and friends.

Subject pronoun	Possessive adjective
You have a bag.	*What's in **your** bag?*
I have a phone.	*It's in **my** bag.*

We can use possessive 's with a possessive adjective and noun.

*This is **my friend's** bag.*

See Grammar focus on page 160.

3 DEVELOP Complete the sentences.

1 (Angela) They're __Angela's__ books. (you) It's __your__ pen.
2 (Daniel) It's _____ phone.
3 (I) This is _____ wallet.
4 (she) Is this _____ bag?
5 (they) That's _____ cat.
6 (we) It's _____ car.
7 (he) These are _____ keys.

4 INTERACT Play the Possessions game.

Is this Ahmed's book? Is this your book? Whose book is this?

5 ASSESS Look at the image. Who is the woman speaking to? Where is she?

6 🔊 **INTEGRATE** Listen. Check your answers from Exercise 5.

7 🔊 **IDENTIFY** Listen to the whole radio show. What things does each person have?

		Tanya	Carlos	Rachel
1	keys	☐	☐	☐
2	phone	☐	☐	☐
3	picture(s)	☐	☐	☐
4	an ID	☐	☐	☐
5	book(s)	☐	☐	☐

LISTENING SKILL Understanding numbers

When listening for numbers, pay attention to the stress. Listen for all parts of the number.

30 → **thir**ty

13 → thir**teen**

31 → thirty-**one**

---

8 🔊 **INTEGRATE** Listen again to the radio show. Complete the sentences with the correct words or numbers.

The radio station is Sunny Radio, ¹_____ FM.

Tanya has ²_____ dollars, ³_____ cents, and ⁴_____ picture of her ⁵_____.

Carlos has ⁶_____ books, ⁷_____ pens, ⁸_____ cents, and ⁹_____ apple.

¹⁰_____ friend is not with her. Rachel doesn't have a bag. The bag is ¹¹_____ friend's bag.

PRONUNCIATION SKILL Pronouncing numbers

🔊 When words have more than one vowel sound, or syllable, one vowel sound is said clearly and loudly. Listen to the difference:

16 → six**teen**

60 → **six**ty

---

9 🔊 **NOTICE** Listen. Choose the vowel sound that is said more clearly and loudly.

1 fif·teen

2 fif·ty

3 sev·en·teen

4 sev·en·ty

5 thir·teen

6 thir·ty

7 eigh·teen

8 eigh·ty

10 🔊 **DEVELOP** Listen and repeat the numbers.

11 WHAT'S YOUR ANGLE? Choose one new thing, one old thing, and one small thing in your bag. Show them to your partner. Do you have the same things?

2.4 Excuse Me...

1 ACTIVATE Discuss the questions in a group.

1 Are you on your phone a lot? Do you use your phone in coffee shops or in class?

2 Do you know someone who is on his or her phone all the time?

3 Is it OK, in your opinion, to use your phone when you are talking to other people?

2 ▶ IDENTIFY Watch the video. As you listen, match the pictures to the sentences.

1 Oh, are you in line? _____

2 Have a great day! _____

3 Hi, can I help you? Uh...hello? Next! _____

4 I'd like one small black coffee and a regular tea, please. _____

5 No problem. It's on me. _____

6 Oh, hi there. Sorry about that! How can I help you? _____

Here are some useful expressions when you are talking to strangers in a restaurant, store, coffee shop, or other public place.

I'd like… and *please* (when you want something)
thanks or *thank you* (when someone gives you something)
you're welcome (after someone says "thank you" to you)
excuse me (to get someone's attention)
sorry (when you do something wrong)

Less polite	More polite
Oh, are you in line?	*Excuse me, are you in line?*
Hey!	*Excuse me…*
I want a coffee.	*I'd like a coffee.*

3 ▶ **ANALZYE** Read the Real-World English box. Watch the video again. Who is polite? Who is not polite? Give an example of something each person says or does that is polite or not polite. Compare your answers with a partner.

4 IDENTIFY Choose the correct polite expression for each conversation.

1 A: I'd like a small pizza, _____.
   B: Sure. That's $10.99.
      a excuse me
      b you're welcome
      ⓒ please

2 A: _____, are you from Brazil?
   B: Yes, I am. Why?
      a Excuse me
      b You're welcome
      c Please

3 A: Here's your order.
   B: _____.
      a Thank you
      b Sorry
      c You're welcome

4 A: Thank you for your help.
   B: _____!
      a That's OK
      b You're welcome
      c Excuse me

5 A: Excuse me, but that's my coffee.
   B: Oh, _____!
      a no problem
      b thanks
      c I'm sorry

6 A: _____ a large tea with milk.
   B: Sure. Here you go.
      a I'd like
      b Give me
      c I want

5 INTEGRATE Work with a partner. Choose a situation and prepare a role play. Use at least two of the polite expressions below.

Excuse me…	I'd like…	Have a nice / great day!	(I'm) Sorry (about that)!	…please
You too!	No problem.	Thanks / Thank you (for…)	It's OK / That's OK.	You're welcome.

Situation 1 Student A: You're in a store. You want a new notebook.
Student B: You're a worker at the store.

Situation 2 Student A: You're at a concert. You're in seat 24A.
Student B: You're at a concert. Someone is in your seat (24A).

Situation 3 Student A: You're a busy server in a coffee shop.
Student B: You're a customer in a coffee shop. You want to order a coffee, but the server is busy.

6 INTERACT Act out your situation for another pair. Give each other feedback. Was everyone polite?

GO ONLINE
to create your own version
of the English For Real video.

2.5 Is It for Me?

1 ACTIVATE Look at the photo. What is in the gift box?
Complete the table with your own ideas.

Possible ✓	Not possible ✗
a cell phone	a bicycle

2 WHAT'S YOUR ANGLE? Imagine your perfect gift is in the
box. What is it?

3 ◀» IDENTIFY Listen to the conversation between two sisters.
Answer the questions.

1 Who is Izzy's gift for?
_____

2 Is it big?
_____

3 Is it expensive?
_____

4 What is the gift?
_____

5 What color is it?
_____

A bride and bridesmaid exchange
gifts in Nha Trang, Vietnam

SPEAKING Asking and answering questions

We use questions with *be* when we want a *yes/no* answer.

A: **Are** they expensive?
B: No, they're not.

We use *wh-* questions when we want more information.

A: **Where** is it from?
B: It's from Portugal.

Make sure you give the right kind of answer to the question. Question words need more
information than *yes/no* questions.

4 INTEGRATE Write five questions to ask about an object. Use these phrases to help you.

Is it (new / for school / etc.)?
What color is it?
How (expensive / big / etc.) is it?

5 INTERACT Play "Twenty Questions." Think of an object from this unit. Your partner asks
questions to guess the object. Switch roles. The only question you can't ask is "What is it?"

Is it something in this room? Is it…?

3 Places

Where is this place? Describe it.

What's your favorite kind of place? Why?

BEHIND THE PHOTO

**REAL-
WORLD
GOAL**

Give someone directions

Think about places you like. Then answer the questions below.

1   What place do you think is beautiful?
2   Why is the place beautiful?
3   Is it a famous place?
4   Is the place new or old?
5   Who do you go there with?
6   What do you do there?
7   What things do you find in that place?

1 ACTIVATE Match each photo with a place. Make a sentence with *this*.

| airport | restaurant | **café** | park | bank | museum | store | supermarket |

 Oxford 3000™

1   This is a bank.

2   _____

3   _____

4   _____

5   _____

6   _____

7   _____

8   _____

2 WHAT'S YOUR ANGLE? For each place in Exercise 1, write the name of a similar place in your city or town.

restaurant: Angelo's Pizza, India Palace
park: Battery Park

GRAMMAR IN CONTEXT *There is...* and *There are...*

We use *There is / There are* to talk about things that are in a place. We use *There is* with singular nouns and *There are* with plural nouns.

There is an airport in my city.
There are many tall buildings in the city.

We use *a, an,* or *one* with *There is* + singular nouns. We don't use *the,* and we don't talk about specific places.

There is one café in our office building. NOT ~~There is the café in our office building.~~

We can use a short form for *There is.*

There's *a lake near the office.*

See Grammar focus on page 161.

3 IDENTIFY Complete the sentences with *There is* or *There are*.

1 _____ten students in the class.
2 _____one English school in the town.
3 _____many children in the park.
4 _____50 states in the United States.
5 _____a phone on the desk.
6 _____a supermarket in the United States called Piggly Wiggly.
7 _____some good stores on this street.
8 _____famous pictures in the museum.

4 INTERACT Look at your list from Exercise 2. Make sentences with *There is* and *There are* about places in your town. Tell a partner.

There are lots of restaurants in my town. One restaurant is Angelo's Pizza.
There's a park in my town and a museum.

5 **ASSESS** Look at the information about a video. Answer the questions.
Then watch the video and check.

1 What do you think the video is about?
   a an airport
   b a company
   c a vacation
2 What do you think the word *headquarters* means?
   a the main office of a company
   b an airport
   c the boss of a big company

✈ Welcome to **BRITISH AIRWAYS Headquarters!**

British Airways
Headquarters

Heathrow Airport

Common nouns describe places, people, and things—for example, *school*, *student*, or *street*.

Proper nouns describe specific places, people, or things. They start with a capital letter.
For example, *Woodward School of English*, *Carlos Arroyo*, or *Bristol Street*.

6 IDENTIFY Read the script. How many different proper nouns can you find? Write a list.

> This is British Airways. It is Britain's biggest airline company. The airline has about 300 planes. They fly to 169 cities around the world.
>
> The British Airways headquarters is near Heathrow Airport in London. The headquarters is called Waterside. It cost 200 million pounds. About 4,000 people work here. It's a very large building—about 9,000 square meters. It is the size of a small town.
>
> There is a street in the center of the building. There are offices on the left and right side. On the street, there is a supermarket and a small shop.* There is also a hairdresser's. There are two cafés. They sell drinks and food. People come here to have a drink and a chat. There is also a large restaurant. The restaurant is by a lake.
>
> * In British English, people say *shop* instead of *store*.

7 DEVELOP Match the proper nouns from the script with the common nouns.

1   headquarters: <u>Waterside</u>
2   a city: _____
3   a country: _____
4   an airline company: _____
5   an airport: _____

8 APPLY Complete the sentences.

1   At the British Airways headquarters, there **is**…
   <u>a supermarket</u>   _____
2   At the British Airways headquarters, there **are**…
   _____   _____

9 ASSESS Read the script again. Are the statements *True* or *False*?

		True	False
1	British Airways is a large company.	✓	☐
2	Its headquarters is in an expensive building.	☐	☐
3	The company has 100 planes that fly to 69 cities around the world.	☐	☐
4	Its headquarters is in a small town called Waterside.	☐	☐
5	Many people work at the British Airways headquarters.	☐	☐
6	There are many places to go inside the building.	☐	☐

10 WHAT'S YOUR ANGLE? In your opinion, is the British Airways headquarters a fun place to work? Why or why not?

In my opinion, the British Airways headquarters is a fun place to work because it's like being in a city. There are many things to do there. Also, it's near a lake, so it's a beautiful place.

3.2 Tips For Travelers

1 ACTIVATE Look at the map. Read the sentences. Find the places on the map.

1 Bondi Beach Public School is **between** Campbell Parade and Gould Street.
2 The Bondi Market is **next to** the school.
3 Bill's restaurant is **on** Hall Street.

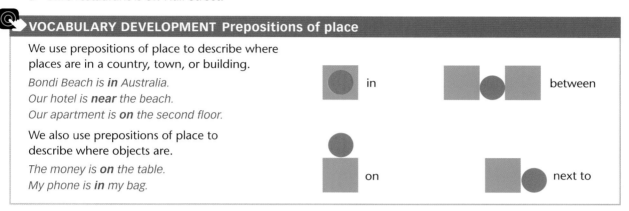

VOCABULARY DEVELOPMENT Prepositions of place

We use prepositions of place to describe where places are in a country, town, or building.

*Bondi Beach is **in** Australia.*
*Our hotel is **near** the beach.*
*Our apartment is **on** the second floor.*

We also use prepositions of place to describe where objects are.

*The money is **on** the table.*
*My phone is **in** my bag.*

in

between

on

next to

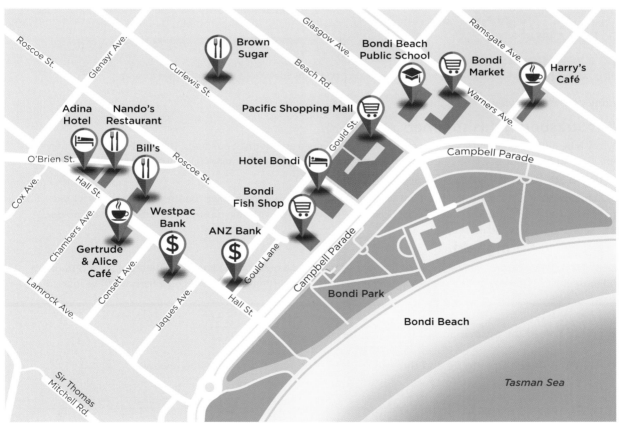

2 USE Work with a partner. Find more places on the map. Use *in*, *on*, *near*, *between*, and *next to* to talk about where places on the map are.

Bondi Park is next to the beach. There is a café on Hall Street.

3 WHAT'S YOUR ANGLE? Write three sentences about where you live. Use prepositions of place.

My house is near the airport. My street is between Howard Street and Edge Street.

GRAMMAR IN CONTEXT Imperatives (commands)

We use the imperative to give advice or directions.

Visit Bondi Beach. It's a fun place.
Walk along Campbell Parade, then *turn* right.

To give someone advice about what *not* to do, we add *don't*.

Don't eat at that restaurant. It's not good. *Try* Bill's Restaurant on Hall Street.

Don't use imperatives in stores or restaurants because they sound rude.

I'd like a coffee, please. NOT ~~Bring me a coffee.~~

See Grammar focus on page 161.

4 DEVELOP Put the words in order to complete the commands.

1 the bank / go / on / Hall Street / to *Go to the bank on Hall Street.*

2 Wairos Avenue / the café / on / try _____

3 the beach / near / at / the hotel / stay _____

4 turn right / on Campbell Parade / don't _____

5 visit / at night / don't / the park _____

6 the new restaurant / dinner / eat / at _____

5 ASSESS Read the online reviews of people's hometowns. Which are positive? ☺ Which are negative? ☹

◦⚬◦ TripTips.us

| Find | | Near | | 🔍 |

Rate your hometown here!
Tell us about the town or city where you're from. Help people decide where to go and what to see!

Today's top three reviews:

Visit Strasbourg this summer! ⚬⚬⚬⚬⚬ *362 reviews*

My city is beautiful. Come and see it! It's popular for its old French and German buildings. There is also a famous university here. Go shopping or sit at a cute café in the center of town. Come in the summer or fall, but don't visit in winter. It's cold!

Enjoy San Juan all year. ⚬⚬⚬⚬⚬ *98 reviews*

My hometown is fun. It's warm and beautiful. Visit our beautiful beaches. Walk down the streets by the colorful, old Spanish houses. Eat Puerto Rican food by the ocean. You'll love it! Listen to Latin music at our fun clubs, too. And don't forget about our parks and museums!

Don't go to Springfield. ⚬⚬⚬⚬⚬ *8 reviews*

I love my hometown—my family and friends are here—but it's not a great place for tourists. There are some restaurants and museums, but the city isn't beautiful. It's near other cities that are interesting. Don't come here. Go there instead!

6 IDENTIFY Read the reviews again. Underline the commands.

7 PLAN Write three things to do and three things *not* to do based on the online reviews.

+	–

8 WHAT'S YOUR ANGLE? Think about your hometown. Take notes.

Include:

- adjectives to describe your town / city
- interesting places for people to visit and things to do
- places not to visit and things not to do

The verb *be* needs to match the subject of the sentence.

I'm *from Cuzco.* *It's* *the old capital of the Inca Empire.*

Use *there is* with singular nouns and *there are* with plural nouns.

There's *a great Chinese restaurant on Main Street.* **There aren't** *any museums in my town.*

9 🔲 **APPLY** Complete the description with the correct form of *be*.

I'm from Cuzco, a city in the Andes Mountains in Peru. It's the old capital of the Inca Empire. There ¹_____ a lot of old Spanish buildings there now, but you can also see parts of the old Inca city. There ²_____ a main square, called the Plaza de Armas, in the center of the city. It ³_____ also the Inca main plaza. In the mountains, there ⁴_____ an old Inca city called Machu Picchu. There ⁵_____ many stone buildings there. Many people come to Cuzco to go there.

There ⁶_____ a lot to do in the city. There ⁷_____ interesting museums. There ⁸_____ also places to buy food on the street. Those ⁹_____ my favorite places to eat! For example, there ¹⁰_____ a market called the Wanchaq Market, which is near the Wanchaq train station and the Garcilaso Stadium.

—Adapted from *The Oxford Companion to Archaeology* (2 ed.) edited by Neil Asher Silberman

10 **WRITE** Write a review of your hometown for *TripTips.us*. Use your notes from Exercise 8.

Use *there is / there are* to describe your town or city.
Use *in, on, near, next to*, and *between* to describe where things are.
Use imperatives for things to do and not to do.
Rate your town from 0–5 stars.

11 **IMPROVE** Read your review. Check it for grammar and spelling mistakes. Make corrections.

Be sure to:
- spell places in town correctly.
- capitalize proper nouns (for example, the names of streets and businesses).
- use *is* with singular nouns and *are* with plural nouns.
- use the correct words to say where things are (*in, on, near, next to, between*).
- use the correct imperative forms.

12 **SHARE** Switch reviews with a classmate. Read your classmate's review. Is his or her hometown interesting?

Macchu Picchu   33

3.3 A Place to Stay

1 ACTIVATE Look at the ad. What is it for?

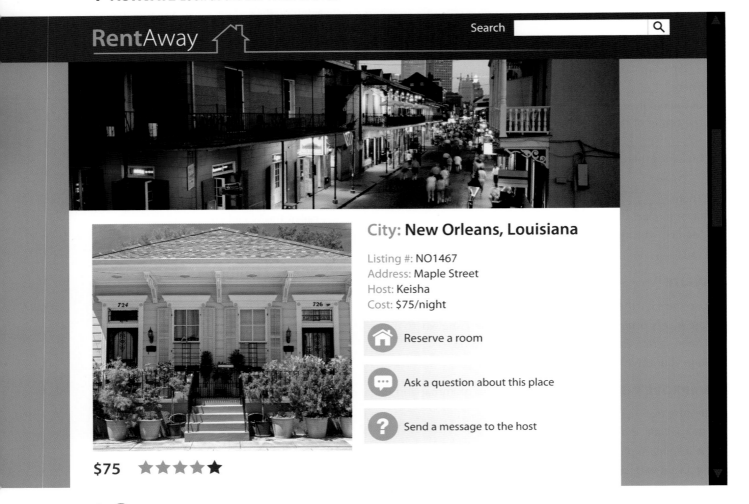

RentAway

Search 🔍

City: New Orleans, Louisiana

Listing #: NO1467
Address: Maple Street
Host: Keisha
Cost: $75/night

🏠 Reserve a room

💬 Ask a question about this place

❓ Send a message to the host

$75 ★★★★★

2 ◀ IDENTIFY Listen to a conversation between two women. Choose the correct answers.

1 The two women are _____.
   a friends   b strangers
2 Melanie is at _____.
   a a hotel   b a person's house
3 Melanie _____.
   a is a tourist   b lives in New Orleans

LISTENING SKILL Understanding why you are listening: Specific information

When you listen, think about what kind of information you need to know. Is it a name, a number, or something else? This will help you focus and understand more.

3 ◀ INTEGRATE Read the questions and find the key words. Then listen again and choose the correct answer.

1 Keisha has a lot of pictures of *the city* / *cats*.
2 Keisha's living room is *big* / *small*.
3 The room is *$100* / *$150* for two nights.
4 Keisha's favorite restaurant is *Bobby's* / *Bubba's*.
5 At the end of the conversation, Keisha gives Melanie a *map* / *key*.

We use *Is there a/an?* / *Are there (any)?* to ask about things in a place. We usually answer *yes/no* questions with short answers.

Is there a dining room in Keisha's house?   No, **there isn't**.
Are there any fun things to do near here?   Yes, **there are**.

We use *There isn't* and *There aren't any* to make negative statements.

There isn't a bathroom in the train station.
There aren't any restaurants on this street.

See Grammar focus on page 161.

4 **APPLY** Complete the questions with *is* or *are*. Add short answers.

1   Is there an office in Keisha's house? _No, there isn't._____

2   ____there a cat in Keisha's house? _____

3   ____there six bedrooms in Keisha's house? _____

4   ____there a kitchen? _____

5   ____there another guest at Keisha's house? _____

6   ____there any good restaurants, parks, and museums in the city? _____

5 **WHAT'S YOUR ANGLE?** Do you use companies like RentAway? Why or why not?

6 **VOCABULARY** Match the names of the rooms to the places in the apartment.

bedroom   kitchen   hall   **dining room**   bathroom   **living room**

⚲ Oxford 3000™

 7 **WHAT'S YOUR ANGLE?** Think about your perfect RentAway apartment.
Where are the rooms? Draw a plan.

8 **INTERACT** Work with a partner. Follow the instructions. Then switch roles.

Student A: You are a RentAway host. Tell your guest about the apartment.

Student B: You are a RentAway guest. Ask questions about the apartment.

3.4 Take a Right!

1 ▶ ACTIVATE Watch the video. Answer the questions.

1 The woman needs to find a *campus building / place to eat*.
2 Max *knows / doesn't know* where the place is.
3 The place is in a *small white / big red* building.

REAL-WORLD ENGLISH Giving directions

When we give directions, we often use commands.

Go straight. ↑

Turn left (onto Main Street). ↰

Take a right (on High Street). ↱

Walk (on/down Main Street). 🚶

We also use our hands to show the directions while we speak.

Sometimes it's rude to use imperatives to tell strangers what to do. But it's not rude to use imperatives when we explain how to do something or give directions or advice.

Rude	Not rude
Go away.	*Cook the rice for 30 minutes.*
Be quiet.	*Walk down this street to get to the beach.*
Don't sit there.	*Take a left onto Hill Street.*
Don't eat on the bus.	*Don't eat at that restaurant! Try this place.*

ENGLISH FOR REAL

2 ▶ **APPLY** Watch the video again. Start at the red X. Follow the directions and draw a line. Write on the map where the shop is and where the University Commons building is.

3 **ANALYZE** Work in groups. Discuss the questions.

1   Do you ask people for directions in the street? How do you ask?
2   Do you ask friends and strangers differently?
3   How do you reply when someone asks you for directions?

4 **INTEGRATE** Look at the map from Exercise 2. Work with a partner. Don't show your partner your map.

Step 1: Choose a place on the map for a special store. Mark it.

Step 2: On a separate page, write directions to the store.

Step 3: Exchange directions with a partner. Follow your partner's directions and mark his or her store on your map.

Step 4: Check with your partner. Are your directions and maps correct?

5 **INTERACT** Work with a partner. Follow the instructions for the role play.

Student A: You are a tourist. Ask your partner directions to a place nearby (for example, a museum, a park, a restaurant).

Student B: A tourist asks for directions to a place nearby. Help the tourist.

Swap roles. Choose new places.

GO ONLINE
to create your own version
of the English For Real video.

37

3.5 What a Great Place!

1 ACTIVATE Look at the pictures. Describe them.

old city	buildings	castle	center of town	water

2 🔊 **ASSESS** Listen to the conversation in a tourist information office.

3 🔊 **INTEGRATE** Choose the correct answer.

1 Helsingor is in *Denmark / England*.
2 The castle in Helsingor is the same castle from *Shakespeare's* Hamlet / *Disney's* Cinderella.
3 The castle is also a *restaurant / museum*.
4 The nice beaches *are / aren't* very near the tourist office.
5 There is a place to rent bikes next to the *beach / train station*.
6 There *is / isn't* a bathroom at the tourist office.

◉▶ PRONUNCIATION SKILL Weak sound of *are* in *there are*

🔊 Listen to the phrase *there are*. Notice how the /r/ sounds blend together.
there are

---

4 🔊 **DEVELOP** Repeat the sentences.

1 There are some nice beaches.
2 There are beautiful old buildings.
3 There are also cafés.
4 There are a lot of people.
5 There are no tall buildings.

5 WHAT'S YOUR ANGLE? Think about a fun or interesting place you know. Write a description (4–5 sentences).

◉▶ SPEAKING Asking where places are

Ask about general places using *Is there...?* or *Are there...?* Use *in, on, next to,* and *near*.
Is there a bathroom **in** this café?   **Are there** parks **near** here?

Ask about where places are with a *yes/no* question or with *Where is/are...?*
Is the dining room on the first floor?   **Where is** the train station?

---

6 INTEGRATE Make a list of 4–5 questions to ask a partner about his or her place.

Are there a lot of people? Where is the art museum?

7 INTERACT Work with a partner. Imagine you work at a tourist office in your interesting place. Your partner is a visitor. Use your ideas from Exercise 5 and 6. Switch roles.

4 Life

What are the people doing?

Is your morning like this?

What do you do every day?

BEHIND THE PHOTO

REAL-WORLD GOAL

Ask someone for the time

1 **How many hours a week do you do these things?**

Work or study: _____
Do chores: _____
Cook and eat: _____
Have fun: _____
Sleep: _____
Total: _____ / 168 hours

2 **Talk with a partner about how many hours a week you do these things.**

4.1 My Famous Family

1 **ACTIVATE** How are the people related? Make sentences using the words.

mother	father	husband	wife	son	daughter	brother	sister

Oxford 3000™

She's his wife. He's their son.

2 **WHAT'S YOUR ANGLE?** Think about a family you know (from TV, a book, or real life). Who is your favorite family member? Why?

The Simpsons are a famous family from TV. My favorite family member is the daughter, Lisa, because she's a good person and she's smart. She's not bad like her brother Bart!

GRAMMAR IN CONTEXT Simple present

We use the simple present to talk about habits and routines.

*I **work** in the morning. I **go** to school in the evening.*

We also use the simple present to talk about facts and opinions.

*The Marches **live** in Concord, Massachusetts. They **love** it there.*

We add *-s* to verbs with *he / she / it*. If the verb ends in *-o*, *-s*, *-x*, *-z*, *-ch*, or *-sh*, we add *-es*.

*Mr. March **works** for the army. His job **finishes** at 2 a.m.*

The verb *have* is irregular.

*They have **four** daughters.*
*She has **blond** hair.*

See Grammar focus on page 162.

3 IDENTIFY Read the description of a family from literature. Find the verbs.

The Marches

Little Women (1868) by Louisa May Alcott tells the story of the March family. The family in the book is similar to the author's life and family. The main character, Jo, is similar to Louisa.

Mrs. March is a busy, happy, kind woman. Her husband, Mr. March, works for the army and is away in the Civil War. She misses her husband, but she isn't lonely. They have four daughters: Jo, Meg, Beth, and Amy. Jo is 15 years old and intelligent. She writes a lot of stories. She wants to be an author. Her sister Meg is 16 and pretty. She wants to have a rich, important husband. Beth is 13. She loves music and wants to be a musician, but she is not strong. She is often sick, too. Amy is 12. She has blond hair and is beautiful.

The family spends a lot of time together. They also spend a lot of time with their neighbors, the Laurence family.

—Adapted from *The Oxford Companion to American Literature* (6 ed.) by James D. Hart and Phillip W. Leininger

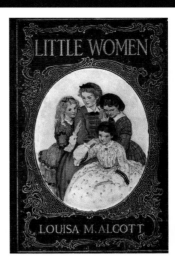

4 ASSESS Answer the questions.

1 What is Mrs. March like? _____
2 How many sisters does Jo have, and what are their names? _____
3 How old is Amy? _____
4 Who loves music? _____
5 Who wants to write books? _____
6 Who are the Marches' neighbors? _____

PRONUNCIATION SKILL /s/, /z/, /iz/ in simple present verbs

🔊 We pronounce the *-s* or *-es* differently depending on the sound that comes before it. Listen for the three different endings.

wants
loves
misses

Words that end with /s/, /z/, /ʃ/, /tʃ/, and /dʒ/ have an extra syllable when *-s* or *-es* is added.

---

5 🔊 NOTICE How many syllables does each word have? Write *1* or *2*. Then listen and check.

1 like _____ likes_____
2 go _____ goes_____
3 choose _____ chooses_____
4 teach _____ teaches_____
5 wash _____ washes_____
6 play _____ plays_____

6 🔊 DEVELOP Listen and repeat.

/s/ works	gets up	likes	wants	sleeps
/z/ lives	goes	needs	spends	listens
/iz/ teaches	finishes	chooses	guesses	fixes

41

7 WHAT'S YOUR ANGLE? Make notes about your family members. Include: name, relationship to you, age, job, and words that describe the person.

Name	Relationship	Age	Job	Description
Gozel	my wife	32	teacher	is kind, has brown hair, loves animals

8 INTERACT Tell a partner about your family. Make sure you use the correct simple present endings.

WRITING SKILL Using *also* and *too*

We use *also* and *too* to add information. Notice where the words are in the sentences.
*My sister likes books. She **also** likes music.*
*I'm from Mexico. My wife is **also** from Mexico.*
*My parents live in Laos. My brother and his family live there, **too**.*

9 PREPARE Rewrite the second sentence. Use *also* or *too*.

1   You have three children? I have three children.
    (too) _____ I have three children, too. _____
2   I have two sisters. I have a brother.
    (too) _____
3   We have a cat. Our neighbors have a cat.
    (also) _____
4   I'm a student. My brothers are students.
    (also) _____
5   My friend's parents are from India. Her husband's parents are from India.
    (too) _____
6   My brother's name is Jeff. My boss's name is Jeff.
    (also) _____

10 WRITE Imagine the people in your family are characters in a book. Write a short description (one paragraph) for the back of the book. Use your notes from Exercise 7.

11 IMPROVE Read your description and check for errors.

Did you…

■ add -s / -es to simple present verbs with *he / she / it*?
■ use *also* and *too* to add information?
■ use capital letters correctly?
■ use the correct form of *be* with each subject?

12 SHARE Switch papers with a partner. How similar are your families?

4.2 How Happy Are You?

1 ACTIVATE Match the verbs with the images to complete the phrases.

spend	have	get up	go	sleep	go	do	get

🔑 Oxford 3000™

_____ early

_____ ready
for work / school

_____ late on
weekends

_____
breakfast / lunch / dinner
with a friend

_____ my
homework

_____ to the
gym

_____ time
with my family

_____ to bed
at 11:00

2 WHAT'S YOUR ANGLE? Write eight sentences about you using the phrases from Exercise 1.

I spend time with my family in the evenings. I have breakfast every morning.

> **READING SKILL Identifying key words: Nouns, verbs, adjectives**
>
> Key words give you important information. Key words can be nouns, verbs, or adjectives.
> noun: *person*
> verb: *makes*
> adjective: *healthy*

3 IDENTIFY Can you find these key words in the survey? Put the words into the correct category in the table.

| great | tired | time | sleep | laugh | gym | friends | help | happy |

Nouns	Verbs	Adjectives
time		

4 INTEGRATE Take the survey.

Search

How Happy Are You?

Take this survey and read our tips!

yes   no

1 Do you sleep 7–9 hours every night?

A tired person is not a happy person.

2 Do you exercise every day?

Find time to go to the gym or walk in the park. It helps you sleep and feel healthy.

3 Do you spend a lot of time with friends?

Make new friends! We all need friends to help us and laugh with us.

4 Do you help people?

Try to help another person every day. It makes you feel good!

5 Do you love what you do or do what you love?

Do you love your job? If not, do you take time to do something you love every day? Try it!

6 Do you get up early?

Studies show that people who get up early in the morning are happy and healthy.

5–6 yes: ☺ Great! You're a very happy person!

3–4 yes: ☺ / ☹ OK. You're happy some days, sad some days. Try to change one thing about your routine.

0–2 yes: ☹ You're not very happy. Read our six tips again. Make changes to your routine!

5 IDENTIFY Read the survey again. Are the statements *True* or *False*?

1 Happy people aren't tired.   True   False
2 Exercise helps you sleep.   True   False
3 Your job is not important to your happiness.   True   False
4 Helping people makes you feel good.   True   False
5 It's good for your health to get up late.   True   False

We form *yes/no* questions in the simple present with *Do / Does* + subject + main verb?
We form short answers with *Yes* + subject + *do/does* or *No* + subject + *don't / doesn't*.

Does the article give good advice?   Yes, it does.
Do you exercise every day?   No, I don't.

See Grammar focus on page 162.

6 APPLY Use the words to write questions.

1   you / get up early   *Do you get up early?*
2   he / go to the gym   _____
3   your friends / spend time together / on weekends   _____
4   you / do your homework / in the evening   _____
5   your roommate / have a job   _____

7 USE Use the verbs from Exercise 1 to write three questions for a partner.

1   _____
2   _____
3   _____

8 INTERACT Read your questions from Exercise 7 to your partner. Your partner will write the questions he / she hears. Switch roles. Check that your partner wrote the questions correctly.

1   _____
2   _____
3   _____

9 WHAT'S YOUR ANGLE? What else makes you happy? Think of two things that aren't on the survey. Write two questions.

10 INTERACT Work with a partner. Ask and answer your questions from Exercise 9. Give short answers and add details.

Do you play sports?
Yes, I do. I play soccer with my friends on weekends.

A soccer game on Kuta Beach, Bali, Indonesia   45

4.3 Be Successful!

1 ACTIVATE Work with a partner. Which things does a successful person do? Add a ✓ or ✗ to the activities.

1 go to work late ☐
2 spend time with family ☐
3 have a lot of free time ☐
4 watch a lot of TV ☐

5 go to bed late at night ☐
6 work on weekends ☐
7 play games at work ☐
8 get up early in the morning ☐

GRAMMAR IN CONTEXT Simple present: Negative forms

We form the simple present negative with subject + *don't* / *doesn't* + verb.

Use *don't* with *I, you, we,* and *they*:
I don't work on Sundays.

Use *doesn't* with *he, she,* and *it*:
He doesn't watch TV.
It doesn't help you.

See Grammar focus on page 162.

2 INTEGRATE Look at the list from Exercise 1. Make sentences about what successful people do and don't do.

A successful person doesn't go to work late. A successful person spends time with her family.

3 IDENTIFY Look at the poster. What is it for?

LISTENING SKILL Contractions (short forms) with *be* and simple present negatives

Negative short forms can be hard to hear when people speak quickly. With the verb *be*, you need to listen for *be + not*. With other simple present negative verbs, you need to listen for *doesn't* or *don't* and the main verb.

I'm not tired.
Chris **isn't** a good worker. **He's not** successful.
He **doesn't go** to work early.
They **don't do** their homework.

4 🔊 IDENTIFY Before you listen to Ray Rich, practice understanding simple present positive and negative forms. Listen to the sentences and choose the form of the verb you hear.

1 positive / negative
2 positive / negative
3 positive / negative
4 positive / negative
5 positive / negative

Ray Rich

Do's and Don'ts for Successful People
Tuesday, November 5
7:00 p.m.
Shea Hall

5 🔊 **ASSESS** Listen to the talk and choose the correct endings to the sentence.

In Ray Rich's opinion, a successful person…

a has a lot of money.

b has a big house.

c has a lot of good friends.

d has an interesting job.

6 🔊 **INTEGRATE** Listen again. What does Ray say? Choose the correct answers.

1 *It's hard / It's not hard* to be successful.

2 He *cleans / doesn't clean* his desk every day.

3 He *works / doesn't work* on Saturdays.

4 He *works / doesn't work* on Sundays.

5 He *talks / doesn't talk* to his friends at the office.

6 He *uses / doesn't use* the Internet at the office.

7 His friends *are / aren't* successful people.

8 He *watches / doesn't watch* TV.

9 TV *is / isn't* good.

7 **WHAT'S YOUR ANGLE?** In your opinion, does Ray give good advice? Why or why not?

VOCABULARY DEVELOPMENT Prepositions of time *on*, *in*, and *at*

Use *in* with times of the day.

in the morning   in the afternoon   in the evening

Use *at* for specific times and with *night*.

at 9 a.m.   at night

Use *on* for days.

on Monday   on weekends   on New Year's Day   on Saturday mornings

The days of the week are:

Monday   Tuesday   Wednesday   Thursday   Friday   Saturday   Sunday

weekend

---

8 🔊 **BUILD** Listen and repeat the days of the week. What's your favorite day of the week? What's your favorite time of day? Tell a partner.

9 **USE** Complete the sentences with *in*, *on*, and *at*. Then make the sentences true for you.

1 He sleeps late _____ weekends.

2 I do housework _____ 2:00 _____ the afternoon.

3 She goes to work _____ 10:00 _____ the morning.

4 We see our friends _____ night.

5 My English class is _____ Mondays, Wednesdays, and Fridays.

10 **INTERACT** Work with a partner. Make a list of three things a successful student does and three things he / she doesn't do. Share with the class.

1 **ACTIVATE** Write the times in numbers.

1   10:00   It's ten.
2 _____   It's eight o'clock.
3 _____   It's five forty-five.
4 _____   It's five to ten.
5 _____   It's quarter to eleven.

6 _____   It's two oh five.
7 _____   It's one thirty.
8 _____   It's ten after four.
9 _____   It's half past three.
10 _____   It's quarter past eleven.

2 **USE** Look at the pictures. Say the time in words.

four fifteen (quarter past four)

1

2

3

4

5

6

3 ▶ IDENTIFY Watch the video. Answer the questions.

1 Max and Andy don't know what time it is because _____.
   a they don't have a clock.
   b the power is out.

2 Max gets _____ from his bedroom to see the time.
   a a watch
   b his phone

3 Max and Andy leave their apartment at _____.
   a 10:10
   b 10:30

4 In class, Kevin asks: _____
   a What time is it?
   b Does anybody have the time?

5 Max tells Kevin that the time is _____.
   a 10:45
   b 11:00

REAL-WORLD ENGLISH Asking for the time

When you ask a stranger for the time, you need to get the person's attention first. Then use a polite question.

Excuse me, do you have the time?
Excuse me! Do you know what time it is?

When asking a friend, you can be more direct.

Hey, what time is it?
What's the time?

4 ▶ ANALYZE Watch the video again. Write down all the questions you hear for asking for the time. Who says them? Compare your answers with a partner.

5 PREPARE Work with a partner. Follow the instructions.

■ Choose a situation: friends or strangers.
■ Choose a time.
■ Write a dialogue about asking for the time. Practice your dialogue.

6 INTERACT Work with another pair. Act out your dialogues for each other. Were they friends or strangers?

GO ONLINE
to create your own version
of the English For Real video.

4.5 A Day in the Life

1 ▶ **ACTIVATE** Look at the pictures. What are Meera's two jobs? Watch the video and check.

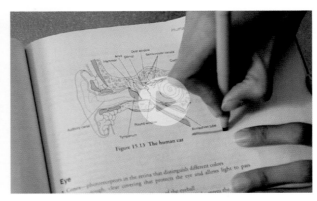

2 **INTEGRATE** Choose the correct answers.

1 Sometimes Meera works in a theater, and sometimes she works in *movies / TV shows*.
2 She starts work at *different times / the same time* every day.
3 At the theater, she starts work at *6 a.m. / 6 p.m.*
4 For tutoring, she works from *3 to 6 / 4 to 7 p.m.*
5 She finishes work *early / late* at the theater.
6 She usually *goes home / goes out with friends* after work.
7 Her favorite thing about being an actor is that every day is *different / fun*.

 SPEAKING Describing habits or routines

Use the simple present tense to talk about things you do (or don't do) every day or every week. Use days and times to say when you do them.

I get up every day at 7. On Monday and Wednesday nights, I take an art class.

---

3 **WHAT'S YOUR ANGLE?** Make notes about your routine.

Monday: start work at 9, finish work at 4 in the afternoon, go to the gym, watch TV, go to bed early

4 **APPLY** Write an activity in each square of the card. Use activities from your daily routine or add others.

5 **INTERACT** Get into groups. Play bingo with the activities on your cards. One person at a time should describe his or her daily routine. The other students cross out the activities on their cards as they hear them. The first one with three activities in a row is the winner.

B I N G O

Now go to page 150 for the Unit 4 Review.

5 Travel

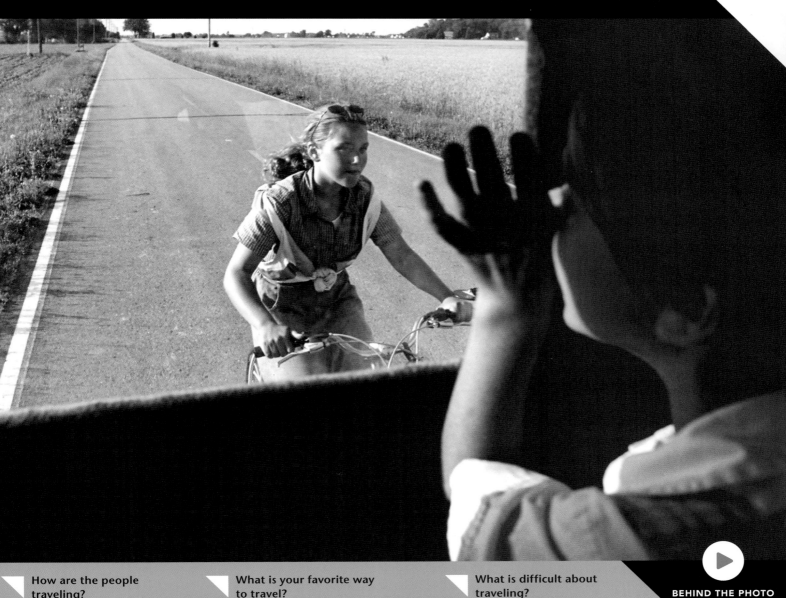

▶ BEHIND THE PHOTO

◤ How are the people traveling?

◤ What is your favorite way to travel?

◤ What is difficult about traveling?

REAL-WORLD GOAL

Buy a ticket from a person (not a machine)

Take the transportation quiz. Then compare your answers with a partner.

1 Where is the José Martí International Airport?
   a Mexico City   b Havana, Cuba   c La Paz, Bolivia

2 Which city does not have a subway system?
   a Stockholm, Sweden   b Tbilisi, Georgia   c Bogotá, Colombia

3 The first airport to be fully powered by solar energy is in what city?
   a Kochi, India   b Melbourne, Australia   c Hamburg, Germany

4 What are the Picasso, the EN Roma, and El Mexicali?
   a boats   b bus lines   c trains

5.1 By Train or by Plane

1 ACTIVATE Match the types of transportation to the images.

by car   by **subway**   by bike   by plane   by boat   by motorcycle   by train   by bus

⚲ Oxford 3000™

I travel _____.

I travel _____.

I travel _____.

I travel _____.

I travel _____.

I travel _____.

I travel _____.

I travel _____.

2 USE Complete the sentences. Use the images in Exercise 1 to help you.

subway   train   motorcycle   plane   bike   car   bus   boat

1   We get on a _____ at the _____ stop on our street.
2   I travel by _____. I leave from the airport.
3   You get on the _____ at the _____ station.
4   Traveling by _____ is good exercise.
5   The _____ travels underground.
6   I like the ocean. I love traveling by _____.
7   Be careful if you travel by _____. There are a lot of cars on the road.

3 WHAT'S YOUR ANGLE? When you travel long distances, do you like to go by car, by train, by plane, or by bus? Why?

I like to go by car because it's convenient.

4 🔊 **IDENTIFY** Listen to the conversation between two friends, Haley and Emma. What is their main reason for traveling?

a   a beach vacation   b   a friend's wedding   c   a business trip

LISTENING SKILL Listening for specific information

> When you need to know something specific, listen for related words. For example, if you need to know the type of transportation someone uses, listen for words like *go*, *travel*, *bike*, and *car*.

5 🔊 **APPLY** Read the sentences. What kind of information is missing? Listen again and complete the sentences.

1   Haley wants to travel by _____.
2   Emma wants to go by _____, but Haley doesn't like the idea.
3   Haley also doesn't like traveling by train because it's slow and _____.
4   They agree to travel by _____ because it's only a _____-hour trip.
5   They also agree to rent _____ and see the _____ when they get there.

GRAMMAR IN CONTEXT Adverbs of frequency

> We use adverbs of frequency with the simple present to say how often we do something.
>
> 100% ◀━━━━━━━━━━━━━━━━━━━━━━━▶ 0%
>
> *always   usually   often   sometimes   never*
>
> Notice the word order.
> I **always** find good deals.   It's **usually** slow and expensive.
> We can use negative verbs with *always*, *usually*, and *often* but not with *sometimes* or *never*.
> I **don't usually drive** on vacation.   I **never travel** anywhere by train.

See Grammar focus on page 163.

6 **INTEGRATE** Put the words in order to make sentences.

1   car / travel / never / by / in the city / I   _____
2   sees her friends / usually / she / in the evenings   _____
3   home / they / for vacation / stay / never   _____
4   often / the countryside / we / visit   _____
5   I / with strangers / English / practice / sometimes   _____
6   always / plane tickets / you / cheap / get   _____

7 **WHAT'S YOUR ANGLE?** Do you agree or disagree with the statements in Exercise 6? Write the sentences so they are true for you.

8 **INTERACT** Share your answers from Exercise 7 with the rest of the class. Do you agree with your classmates? Discuss.

5.2 I Hate Driving Here!

1 **ACTIVATE** How do you learn about things happening in your community? Share your ideas with a partner.

My city has a website. I often talk to my neighbors.

2 **IDENTIFY** Read the opinions from readers of the *San Pedro Sun*. Find something positive (+) and something negative (–) in each reader's opinion.

The San Pedro Sun

Readers respond to yesterday's story "Mayor asks:
What do you think of the public transportation in our town?"

I usually love riding my bike, but it's difficult in this town. For example, there are always a lot of cars on the main streets, and there is no place for bikers to ride. Also, the drivers don't watch for people on bikes. It's dangerous! We need a bike path.

👤 *Dana Smith*

I love taking the subway for many reasons. For example, the station is clean, and the trains are clean, too. They're also fast, and the drivers are always nice. I usually take the bus or walk to the subway station. I don't always like taking the bus because it's sometimes late and a bit slow, but it's OK.

👤 *Marlon Jimenez*

I love our town. We have great transportation. For example, the subway and the buses are excellent. But I hate driving here these days. There are a lot of cars now! I hate sitting in my car and waiting at every red light. We need to try something different—maybe hot air balloon taxis that fly over the cars! 😃

👤 *Heidi Fleischer*

3 **IDENTIFY** Read the article again. Are the statements *True* or *False*?

1	Dana has a bike.	True	False
2	Dana loves cars.	True	False
3	There are a lot of cars in San Pedro.	True	False
4	Marlon usually takes the subway.	True	False
5	The buses are sometimes late.	True	False
6	Heidi drives a car.	True	False
7	Heidi has a hot air balloon.	True	False

4 🔊 **VOCABULARY** Choose the correct travel verbs. Then listen and check.

1 A lot of people *ride / drive* their bikes to work, but it's often dangerous to *bike / fly* in the city.
2 Some people *drive / sail* their car downtown, but there's usually a lot of traffic.
3 I usually *walk / take* to the subway station, and then I *take / drive* the train to the office.
4 Sometimes I *take / walk* the bus to class.
5 When I *ride / fly* the train, it's nice to look out the window.
6 On weekends, we often *sail / fly* our boat on the lake.
7 When I travel from the United Kingdom to the United States, I usually *fly / sail* with British Airways.

5 **USE** Use each verb in a sentence that is true for you.

ride	sail	fly	take	drive	walk	bike

 Oxford 3000™

I never bike in the city.

GRAMMAR IN CONTEXT *like / love / hate* + a verb in the *-ing* form

We can use the *-ing* form of a verb as a noun. We can use it after *like*, *love*, or *hate*.

*I love my bike. I usually love rid**ing** my bike.*
*I don't like planes. Do you like fly**ing**?*

If a verb ends in *-e*, drop the *-e* before adding *-ing*.

*bike → bik**ing***
*take → tak**ing***

If a short verb ends in one vowel + one consonant, double the consonant before adding *-ing*.

*run → ru**nn**ing*
*swim → swi**mm**ing*
*get → ge**tt**ing*

See Grammar focus on page 163.

6 **WHAT'S YOUR ANGLE?** Put an emoticon next to each activity to show how you feel about it: love ❤, like ☺, don't like ☹, or hate ☹. Then add two of your own activities.

1

2

3

4

5

6

7 INTEGRATE Use your answers from Exercise 5. Write questions that you can ask a partner about what he / she likes doing.

Do you like biking?

8 INTERACT Work with a partner. Take turns asking and answering your questions from Exercise 7.

> **WRITING SKILL Using *for example***
>
> We often give examples to support our ideas. Before an example or a list of examples, we can use the phrase *for example*. Put a comma after the phrase.
>
> *I love taking the subway for many reasons.* **For example,** *the station is clean, and the trains are clean, too.*

9 INTERACT Work with a partner. Read each sentence. Then write a second sentence using *for example*.

1 There are different ways to travel around Europe.

   For example, there are airports in many cities.

2 I do a lot on Saturdays.

   _____

3 There are many ways to get around our town.

   _____

4 The students in our school are from different places.

   _____

5 Some people *hate* living in the city for many reasons.

   _____

6 Other people *love* living in the city for many reasons.

   _____

10 WHAT'S YOUR ANGLE? Think about the transportation in your town or city. Write 1–2 positive (+) examples. Why do you like them? Write 1–2 negative (–) examples. What are the problems?

Positive (+)	Negative (–)
The subway station is clean.	The bus is sometimes slow.

11 INTEGRATE Write comments for your town or city's website. Tell the mayor what you think of the transportation. Use your notes from Exercise 10 and the model text on page 54 to help you.

12 IMPROVE Check your comments for errors.

Did you…
- spell the transportation words correctly?
- correctly use *like / love / hate* + a verb in the *-ing* form?
- include frequency words (*usually, sometimes,* etc.)?
- use *for example* to give examples?

13 SHARE Exchange comments with a classmate and check his or her work. Do you have similar opinions?

5.3 Do You Share?

1 ACTIVATE Discuss with the class. How do you find each of these?

1 a good restaurant
2 a plane ticket
3 a ride to the airport
4 things to do in a city

2 WHAT'S YOUR ANGLE? What apps or websites do you use when you travel? What do they do?

> **READING SKILL Using headings**
>
> Headings tell you what each part of a text is about. Look at the headings to find out what information is in a text and how the information is organized.

3 ASSESS Before you read the article, look at the headings.

1 How many sections are there?
2 What is section 1 about?
3 Which section is about food?
4 Which section is about transportation?

The "Sharing Economy"
New Possibilities for Travelers

What is the "sharing economy"?

Services like Citi Bike, Zipcar, and Airbnb are very popular now.

People and companies use the Internet to share bikes, cars, and rooms.

Where do you stay?

Some travelers don't go to hotels. They stay with local people for free through sites like CouchSurfing.com. Other companies like HomeAway connect travelers to people with a room or house to rent.

How do you get around?

Ride-sharing apps help drivers and riders connect. Some are free, like Hitch-a-Ride. Others are pay services, like Lyft and Uber. Car-sharing companies like Zipcar let you use a car for a few hours. These services are great for travelers who don't have their cars with them or for people who don't want to buy a car.

Many cities, such as Shanghai, Mexico City, and Paris, also offer bike-sharing programs. It's cheap, easy, and fun!

Where do you eat?

There are even meal-sharing apps now! Sites like EatWith help local cooks share food with tourists in their homes. It's definitely more interesting than a restaurant!

4 **IDENTIFY** Read the whole article. Choose the correct answers.

1 *Sharing* means _____.
   a selling something to a person
   b more than one person using the same thing

2 It's more expensive to _____.
   a stay in a hotel
   b go "couch surfing"

3 _____ is an example of a free service.
   a Hitch-a-Ride
   b HomeAway

4 The article says that _____ are great for people who don't want to buy cars.
   a taxis and buses
   b Zipcar and Lyft

5 You can use a _____ to try food in another country.
   a ride-sharing app
   b meal-sharing app

VOCABULARY DEVELOPMENT Agent nouns: Verb + -er and noun + -ist

When you add the ending *-er* to a verb, the word becomes a noun. It means "a person who does ____."

verb   *noun*
write   **writer** (a person who writes)

We sometimes add the ending *-ist* to a noun to make a new noun that means "a person who does or studies ___." We often use this form for people who do something as a hobby or a job.

noun (thing)   *noun (person)*
science   **scientist** (a person who studies or works in science)

---

5 **IDENTIFY** Find the four agent nouns in the reading.

6 **INTEGRATE** Complete the chart with the nouns meaning "people who do things."

	+ -er		**+ -ist**
someone who **teaches**	teacher	someone who works in **science**	
someone who **rides**		someone who makes **art**	
someone who **travels**		someone who rides a **motorcycle**	
someone who **drives** (a car, bus, etc.)		someone who takes **tours** of new places	

7 **WHAT'S YOUR ANGLE?** What agent nouns can you use to describe yourself?

Sometimes I'm a traveler. I'm also a good writer and a soccer player.

GRAMMAR IN CONTEXT The simple present: Wh- questions

For all verbs apart from *be*, we form *wh-* questions in the simple present with:

Question word + *do / does* + subject + verb?
Where do you stay?

Question words get more information than a *yes/no* question.
How do you get around? With a bike-sharing service.
Where does he usually eat? At a friend's house.

See Grammar focus on page 163.

8 INTEGRATE Write questions. Then use the article to add answers.

1 when / people / use Zipcar

   When do people use Zipcar?   *when they need a car for a few hours*

2 what / people and companies / use the Internet for

   _____   _____

3 what services / people / use for ride sharing

   _____   _____

4 why / people / use bike-sharing services

   _____   _____

5 what / sites like HomeAway / do

   _____   _____

6 how much / CouchSurfing.com / cost

   _____   _____

7 where / tourists / eat / with meal-sharing apps

   _____   _____

PRONUNCIATION SKILL Falling intonation in *wh-* questions

🔊 A speaker's pitch often rises at the end of a *yes/no* question:

Do you have a car?

In a *wh-* question, the pitch usually rises on the most important word and then falls:

What ride-sharing app do you use?

How much does it cost?

Listen to the example sentences. Notice where the pitch rises and falls.

---

9 🔊 DEVELOP Look at the sentences. Guess where the pitch rises. Then listen and repeat.

1 What sharing services do you use?
2 Where do you usually stay on vacation?
3 Do you like ride sharing?
4 What is your favorite travel app?
5 How do you find a good restaurant?

10 INTERACT With a partner, take turns asking and answering the questions from Exercise 9. Ask for more information.

A: What sharing services do you use?
B: I use Uber and Citi Bike.
A: How much does Citi Bike cost?

A woman rides her electric bike in Rome, Italy

1 ACTIVATE When do you have problems understanding people? Do you ask them to repeat things? What do you usually say?

I don't understand people when they speak fast. I say, "Can you speak slowly, please?"

2 ▶ IDENTIFY Watch the video. Answer the questions.

1   Max and Andy are at _____.
    a   the bus station   b   the train station   c   the airport

2   Max doesn't hear Andy because he is listening to _____.
    a   music   b   a podcast   c   an audio book

3   Andy has Max's _____.
    a   ID   b   ticket   c   bag

4   At first, their train is leaving from track _____.
    a   64   b   5   c   6

5   Their train is now at track _____.
    a   66   b   6   c   7

3 ▶ ANALYZE Read the Real-World English box. Then watch the video again. Answer the questions.

1   Which expressions does Max use to ask Andy to repeat something?
2   Which expression does Andy use with the station attendant?
3   Why? What is different about them?

With friends, you can be direct when you want them to repeat something.

Huh?   What?   Say that again?   I'm sorry, what?

With teachers, bosses, and people you don't know well, you need to use longer, less direct questions.

Sorry, could you repeat that?   Could you say that again, please?

You can also use a question word for specific information.

A: The meeting is at 3:30.
B: I'm sorry, what time?

When people repeat the information, they don't usually repeat their statement exactly, or they repeat only the most important information.

Repeating in different words

A: Do you have the tickets?
B: Yeah, they're here.
A: What?
B: I said I have them.

Repeating only the most important information

Andy: My mom loves cooking for guests.
Max: Huh? What?
Andy: I said my mom loves cooking.

4 **PREPARE** Look at the three situations. Make notes about what Student A might say in each situation.

Situation 1 Student A: You are a student. You meet a new student from another country. You ask the person questions about himself/herself.

Student B: You don't understand your classmate's English very well, but you want to answer the questions!

Situation 2 Student A: You are at a bus station. You ask the station attendant what time the next bus to the city leaves.

Student B: You are a station attendant at a bus station. The buses are very noisy, and sometimes you don't hear the customers' questions.

Situation 3 Student A: You want to find a good place in your city for lunch. You ask a friend for directions, but you can't hear them clearly.

Student B: Tell your friend a good place in your city to go for lunch. Give directions.

5 **INTERACT** Work with a partner. Role-play one of the situations using your notes from Exercise 4. Student A begins the conversation.

6 **ANALYZE** Think about your conversation from Exercise 5. Discuss the questions with your partner.

1   How did you ask for information?
2   How did you ask your partner to repeat something?
3   How did you repeat the information for your partner?
4   Why did you choose those words?

7 **INTERACT** Work with a new partner. Choose a different situation from Exercise 4 to role-play.

GO ONLINE
to create your own version
of the English For Real video.

5.5 A Ticket to Somewhere

1 ◀)) **ACTIVATE** Listen to the conversations. Fill in the missing information on the tickets.

A

Toowoomba to Brisbane

Saturday, 19 November
Leaves ¹_____ a.m.
Arrives 11:40 a.m.
Brisbane to Toowoomba
Sunday 20 November
Leaves ²_____ p.m.
Arrives 4:20 p.m.
Price: ³_____

B

 Train Ticket

Montréal, QC — Toronto, ON

Leaves: ⁴_____ p.m.

Arrives: ⁵_____ p.m.

Price: ⁶_____

2 **ASSESS** Which ticket is one way? Which is round trip? What's the difference?

3 ◀)) **IDENTIFY** What information is repeated?

1 Conversation A   _____

2 Conversation B   _____

4 **WHAT'S YOUR ANGLE?** Do you travel by bus or by train more often? Why?

I travel by bus more often because it's cheap, but I like traveling by train, too.

SPEAKING Buying tickets

Some helpful phrases to use when buying a ticket are:

I'd like…	*a bus ticket*
I need…	*a round-trip train ticket to [place] at [time]*
How much is…?	*a one-way plane ticket*

---

5 **PREPARE** Think of a place you would like to visit. When do you want to go?
How do you want to travel there? Make notes.

6 **INTERACT** Role-play with a partner. Buy a bus, plane, or train ticket using your notes from
Exercise 5. Ask for repetition of at least one piece of information. Then switch roles.

6 Skills

| What is the boy doing? | What are you good at? | What are three skills children learn? | BEHIND THE PHOTO |

Which skills would you like to have or learn? Rank them from 1–10.
Add one of your own.

_____ art   _____ music

_____ sports   _____ language

_____ math   _____ science

_____ cooking   _____ writing

_____ teaching   _____ computers   other _____

REAL-WORLD GOAL

Start a conversation
with a person you
don't know well

1 ACTIVATE Add the verbs to the image to describe abilities.

| see | draw | paint | speak | jump | climb | remember |

⚲ Oxford 3000™

1 _____ many
languages

2 _____ a wall

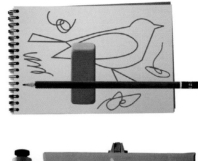

3 _____ or
_____ a beautiful picture

4 _____ things from
far away

5 _____ information

6 _____ high

2 🔊 USE Match the sentence halves. Listen and check.

1	Street artists	a	draw pictures of superheroes.
2	Basketball players	b	speak many languages.
3	Rock climbers	c	remember important information from class.
4	Translators	d	paint on the wall.
5	Comic book artists	e	jump high and run a lot.
6	Good students	f	climb mountains.

GRAMMAR IN CONTEXT *Can / can't* for ability

We use *can* and *can't* to talk about our abilities. We use a verb after *can* and *can't*.

*We **can speak** English.*
*Cats **can't fly**.*

See Grammar focus on page 164.

3 INTEGRATE Use the abilities from Exercise 1 and the prompts to write sentences.

1 speak many languages / she / + *She can speak many languages.*
2 speak many languages / she / – *She can't speak many languages.*
3 run / I / +
4 fly / I / –
5 climb trees / the children / +
6 swim / he / –
7 remember phone numbers / we / –
8 dance / you / +

 PRONUNCIATION SKILL *Can / can't*

In American English, *can* and *can't* sound similar when used alone or in short answers. The *t* in *can't* is not always pronounced clearly.

*You **can't**?*
*Yes, I **can**.*

Can and *can't* sound very different in statements. Listen to the vowel sounds. Listen for the words that are stressed.

*He can **sing**.*	*I can play **tennis**.*	*What can you **do**?*
*He **can't** dance.*	*I **can't** play soccer.*	*What **can't** you do?*

4 ◀⁾ **NOTICE** Listen and repeat the sentences.

5 PREPARE Choose *can* or *can't* to make true sentences about you.

1 I *can / can't* dance.
2 I *can / can't* play the guitar.
3 I *can / can't* do math.
4 I *can / can't* drive.
5 I *can / can't* cook.
6 I *can / can't* play tennis.
7 I *can / can't* speak three languages.
8 I *can / can't* run five miles.
9 I *can / can't* ride a bike.
10 I *can / can't* draw.

6 INTERACT Work with a partner. Student A, read your sentences from Exercise 5. Student B, make a note of which activities Student A can and can't do. Check your answers and then switch roles.

A street musician in Rome, Italy

 7 WHAT'S YOUR ANGLE? Think of a superhero you know from comic books, movies, or TV shows. What is his or her superpower? What *can't* he or she do? Tell a partner.

Spider-Man can jump high and climb buildings. He can't fly.

8 IDENTIFY Read the text. What skill does each person have?

Three Real People with SUPERPOWERS

Bat

2 Daniel Kish (1966–), "Batman"

Daniel Kish can't see, but he can ride a bike! He uses echolocation. This means that he makes sounds and listens for the echo to "see" what's around him. This is what bats* do when they fly at night.

1 Beth Rodden (1980–), Mountain climber

Most people can't climb like Beth Rodden! She is a champion rock climber. She can climb a mountain as easily as you or I climb the stairs. She climbed a mountain in California that no one climbed again!

3 Stephen Wiltshire (1974–), British artist

Stephen Wiltshire can see something once and remember all the details. He can draw a perfect picture of a city. He created a picture of Tokyo that was 30 feet (10 meters) long after a 30-minute helicopter ride.

READING SKILL Taking notes with important words

Taking notes can help you understand and remember information in a text. Write important words like names, numbers, and dates.

9 INTEGRATE Read again. Take notes with important words from the article.

1 Person 1: _____

2 Person 2: _____

3 Person 3: _____

10 ASSESS Read the article again. Are the statements *True* or *False*?

1 Beth Rodden can climb mountains.	True	False
2 Beth Rodden was born in 1966.	True	False
3 Daniel Kish can see things from far away.	True	False
4 Daniel Kish is also known as "Spider-Man."	True	False
5 Stephen Wiltshire is more than 40 years old.	True	False
6 Stephen Wiltshire remembered all the details of Tokyo after seeing it for 30 minutes from a helicopter.	True	False
7 Stephen Wiltshire is American.	True	False

11 WHAT'S YOUR ANGLE? Which superpower is most interesting to you? Why?

12 INTERACT Work in groups. Think of a new superhero. Write four sentences about him or her. Include the hero's name, two things he or she can do (superpowers), and one thing he or she can't do.

6.2 Amira Online

1 ACTIVATE Work in groups. What social media do you use? Do you use it often? What do you use it for?

I usually post my vacation photos on Instagram.
I check Facebook every day!

2 VOCABULARY Match the activities to the images.

play computer games	play the guitar	sing a song
take photos	play tennis	play basketball

 Oxford 3000™

3 USE Write the activity or activities.

1 You do this activity with a camera: _____

2 These activities are sports: _____,
_____

3 These activities are related to music: _____,
_____

4 You can do this activity at home, on the Internet, or on your smartphone:
_____

4 ASSESS Read the social media post. Answer the questions.

1   What does Amira love doing?
2   What does she hate?
3   What can she do?
4   Where are her friends from?
5   What can't she do?

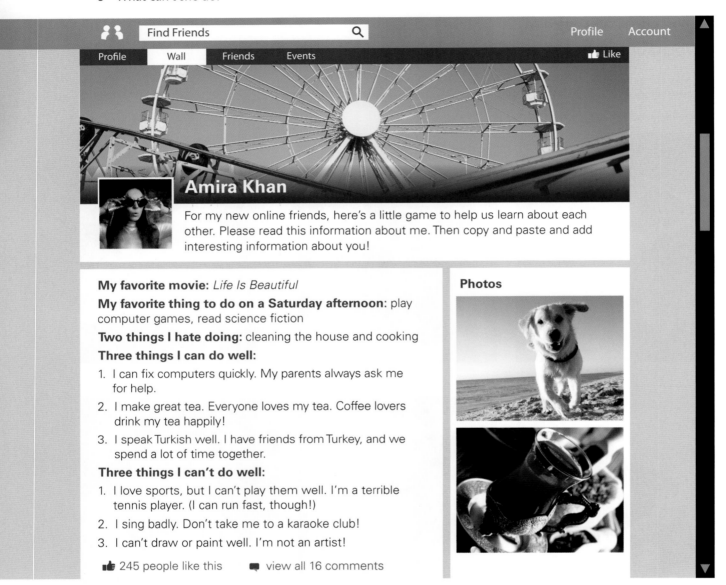

My favorite movie: *Life Is Beautiful*

My favorite thing to do on a Saturday afternoon: play computer games, read science fiction

Two things I hate doing: cleaning the house and cooking

Three things I can do well:

1. I can fix computers quickly. My parents always ask me for help.
2. I make great tea. Everyone loves my tea. Coffee lovers drink my tea happily!
3. I speak Turkish well. I have friends from Turkey, and we spend a lot of time together.

Three things I can't do well:

1. I love sports, but I can't play them well. I'm a terrible tennis player. (I can run fast, though!)
2. I sing badly. Don't take me to a karaoke club!
3. I can't draw or paint well. I'm not an artist!

👍 245 people like this   💬 view all 16 comments

GRAMMAR IN CONTEXT Adverbs of manner

We use adverbs of manner to talk about how we do things. We form most adverbs by adding *-ly* to an adjective. For adjectives that end in *y*, change the *y* to an *i*.

*quick → Amira fixes computers **quickly**.*
*bad → She sings **badly**.*
*happy → We **happily** take photos and post them on Instagram.*

Some adverbs are irregular and don't end in *-ly*.

*good → I can't speak Spanish **well**.*
*fast → You walk very **fast**!*

See Grammar focus on page 164.

5 IDENTIFY Find seven sentences with adverbs of manner in Amira's post.

6 INTEGRATE Write the adverb for each adjective to complete the sentences.

1 (beautiful) They play the piano _beautifully_.
2 (quiet) He works _____.
3 (angry) The teacher speaks _____.
4 (fast) You walk_____.
5 (good) He dances_____.
6 (loud) She speaks_____.
7 (careful) I always drive_____.

7 WHAT'S YOUR ANGLE? Make notes about yourself. What things do you do well? What things do you do badly? Share with a partner.

8 WRITE Write a social media post like Amira's. Fill in your own information.

Profile	Wall	Friends	Events		👍 Like

My favorite movie:
My favorite thing to do on a Saturday afternoon:
Two things I hate doing:
Three things I can do well:
1.
2.
3.
Three things I can't do well:
1.
2.
3.

WRITING SKILL Checking your work: Word order

Make sure that your sentences use correct word order. Adverbs of manner usually come after the verb. If there's an object, the adverb comes after the object.
I speak French well but German badly.

Adverbs of frequency usually come before the verb unless the verb is *be*.
I usually practice French with my friends, but I never practice German.
I'm always tired in the morning.

---

9 INTEGRATE Find and correct the errors.

1 Maya sings beautifully opera.   _Maya sings opera beautifully._
2 I well can paint pictures.   _____
3 My sister can't fast swim.   _____
4 Our neighbor speaks well Korean.   _____
5 Safely we ride always our bikes.   _____
6 Always the students talk loudly.   _____
7 Karim badly plays soccer.   _____

10 IMPROVE Read your post.

Did you...

- put all the words in the correct order?
- use adverbs to talk about how you do things?
- spell the adverbs correctly?

11 SHARE Exchange papers with a partner. Check his or her work.

6.3 Are You a Polymath?

1 ACTIVATE Do you recognize these people from history? Why are they famous?

| inventor | artist | thinker | writer | doctor |

... is a famous...

Leonardo da Vinci

Benjamin Franklin

Avicenna (Ibn Sina)

GRAMMAR IN CONTEXT *Yes/no* questions with *can*

To make questions with *can*, we change the order of the subject and *can*: *Can* + subject + verb?

Can *Usain Bolt run fast?*
Can *you speak Italian?*

We don't repeat the other verb in the short answer.

*Yes, he **can**!*
*No, I **can't**.*

See Grammar focus on page 164.

2 DEVELOP Write questions using *can* and the prompts.

1 the teacher / read and write Mandarin _____
2 you / do math _____
3 Lady Gaga / sing _____
4 Brazilians / speak Portuguese _____
5 you / write music _____
6 your friend / draw beautiful pictures _____

3 INTERACT Work with a partner. Take turns asking and answering the questions from Exercise 2.

4 🔊 **IDENTIFY** Listen to the introduction to a radio interview. What is a *polymath*? Are you a polymath? Do you know a polymath?

LISTENING SKILL Recognizing statements as questions

You know how to recognize questions by the word order:

Can *you **sing** well?*

In spoken English, sometimes a statement can also be a question. You can recognize this kind of question by the speaker's intonation. The speaker's pitch goes up at the end of a statement used as a question.

🔊 Listen to the two sentences. Notice how the pitch rises in the second sentence.

I can speak Spanish.   *You can speak Spanish?*

We often use this kind of question when we're surprised by something.

5 🔊 **NOTICE** Listen. Choose *statement* or *question*.

1 statement question   4 statement question
2 statement question   5 statement question
3 statement question   6 statement question

6 🔊 **INTEGRATE** Listen to the second part of the radio show. Complete the questions that the interviewer asks.

1 _What_ do you _teach_ at the university?
2 _____ you _____ an instrument?
3 You _____ in concerts?
4 Where _____ you _____?
5 _____ you _____ many languages?
6 You _____ *six* languages?
7 _____ you also _____?
8 You _____ a book out, too?
9 _____ you good at _____?

7 🔊 **IDENTIFY** Choose all the correct answers.

1 Mira is good at…
   a math   b languages   c writing   d sports   e cooking
2 Mira can play…
   a the violin   b the flute   c the guitar   d the piano   e the drums
3 Mira can speak…
   a Russian   b Spanish   c Chinese   d German   e Japanese

◉ VOCABULARY DEVELOPMENT Adjective + *at* + noun

One way to talk about your skills is with an adjective + *at* + an activity.
She's great at math.
I'm good at languages.
I'm terrible at sports.
He's bad at singing.

---

8 WHAT'S YOUR ANGLE? What are you good at? great at? bad at? terrible at? Write four sentences.

I'm good at running. I'm great at drawing.

9 USE Work with a partner. Follow the model. Take turns.

A: Are you good at math?
B: No, I'm terrible at math!
A: You can't be a banker.

Activities	Jobs
math	artist
driving	chef
cooking	video game developer
drawing	banker
programming computers	race car driver

10 WHAT'S YOUR ANGLE? Make a list of five interesting things you can do. Then take a survey of your classmates. Try to find one person who can do each thing that you can do.

6.4 How about You?

1 ACTIVATE How do you start a conversation with someone you don't know? How about someone you know? How do you keep the conversation going? Brainstorm ideas with a partner.

2 ANALYZE Which questions are appropriate to ask a person you don't know well? Which are not appropriate? Why? Discuss with the class.

	Good conversation starter	Bad conversation starter
1 So, what do you study?	☐	☐
2 So, what's your religion?	☐	☐
3 Do you like sports?	☐	☐
4 Are you married?	☐	☐
5 What do you do for work?	☐	☐
6 How much money do you make?	☐	☐

3 ▶ IDENTIFY Watch the video. Who is better at keeping the conversation going? Why do you think so?

There are several ways to keep a conversation going. You can:

- ask about the other person after giving information about yourself:

  A: *I'm from Madrid.* **How about you?** / **What about you?** / **And you**?

- respond with interest and ask for more details:

  A: *I love Russian literature.*

  B: **Really?** / **Interesting.** / **What do you like about it?** / **Who's your favorite author**?

- look for something in common:

  A: *Do you like soccer?*

  B: *No, not really. I prefer baseball.*

  A: **Oh, I like baseball, too!**

You can change the subject and ask a new question if the conversation stops:

So… you study business, right?

4 ▶ **IDENTIFY** Watch the video again. Write two questions Max asks to keep the conversation going. Write two questions Kevin asks.

5 **INTEGRATE** Choose a topic. Think of three questions to ask someone you don't know very well.

So, do you like traveling? What's your favorite place to travel? Why do you like it?

6 **INTERACT** Work with a partner. Imagine you don't know each other very well. Follow the instructions.

You are in a coffee shop.

Student A, start a conversation with Student B.

Student B, keep the conversation going.

If the conversation stops, change the subject.

Keep the conversation going as long as you can.

7 **ANALYZE** Discuss with your partner. How well did you keep the conversation going? What can you do better? Use the information in the skill box to help you.

GO ONLINE
to create your own version
of the English For Real video.

6.5 I Can Do That!

1 ACTIVATE Read the job ads. What skills does a person need to do each job? Make notes.

1

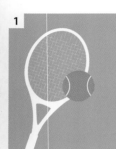

Coaches and Tutors Needed

Lakeside School needs new coaches for volleyball, tennis, and softball.
Many Lakeside students also need extra help with math and reading.

email principal Fred Williams:
fwilliams@Lakeside.sch

2

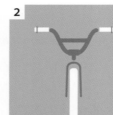

Billie's Bike Tours

Become a tour guide. Show tourists the city by bike!
Great exercise, good money.
Language skills a plus.

Call Billie at 333-404-2121

3

Now hiring: singers, dancers, and musicians for our big Saturday night show.

Must be familiar with many different styles of music!
Center Stage Restaurant, 171 Main Street
Come in for an audition on Saturday, May 5, at 11 a.m., or send us your video.

4

Games Games Games!

Are you good with computers? Do you like games? We make and sell games of all kinds.
We need people in our office. Help us make or test our games!
We also need people in our store.
Help us sell games!
Click here to apply on our website.

2 ▶ IDENTIFY Watch the audition and look at the ads from Exercise 1. Which job does the man want? Does he have all of the skills?

3 ▶ IDENTIFY Watch again. Choose the correct answers.

1 Emiliano is _____ years old.
   a 23   b 24

2 He _____ play different kinds of music.
   a can   b can't

3 He _____ dance flamenco.
   a can   b can't

4 Emiliano _____ plays music.
   a often   b always

5 Near the end of the video, Emiliano plays his own song, called _____.
   a "I Can Have"   b "I Can't Have"

4 WHAT'S YOUR ANGLE? Choose one of the job ads. Read the information in the Speaking box below. Make notes on which skills and abilities you have for the job.

▶ SPEAKING Talking about abilities

There are different ways to talk about your abilities. You can use *be* and *be good / bad at*:

I'm funny.   *I'm a good singer.*   *I'm good at math.*

You can use *can* + verb:

I can cook well.   *I can't work on weekends.*

You can use *have*:

I have computer skills.   *I don't have superpowers.*

Using a variety of phrases makes you sound more interesting and confident.

5 INTERACT Work with a partner. Imagine you are making an "audition video" for the job you want. Introduce yourself and explain why you are great for the job.

6 INTERACT Listen to your partner's "audition video." Take notes about his or her skills and abilities. Ask some follow-up questions.

7 Reasons

Why are the people there?

What do you like to talk about and why?

Why do people enjoy talking?

BEHIND THE PHOTO

REAL-WORLD GOAL

Apologize to someone

1 Answer the questions about yourself. Think about your reasons for doing things.

1 Why do you study English?

2 Do you like the place where you live now? Why (or why not)?

3 What time do you usually get up during the week? Why?

4 What do you do for exercise? Why?

5 Where do you want to travel next? Why?

2 Share your answers with a partner.

7.1 Come Rain or Shine

1 ACTIVATE Look at the images. What is the weather like?

It's warm. The sun is out. There are gray clouds in the sky.	The weather is bad. There's a lot of rain and wind.	There's a lot of snow. It's cold. It's nice and cool.	It's hot!

🔑 Oxford™ 3000

1 _____
_____
_____

2 _____

3 _____

4 _____   5 _____

2 VOCABULARY What kind of weather do you like? What do you like doing in this kind of weather?

I like cold days with a lot of snow. I like staying at home and reading.

3 WHAT'S YOUR ANGLE? Look at the photos. Which is your favorite? Why?

 YOURPHOTOS

Profile   Photos   Sign out

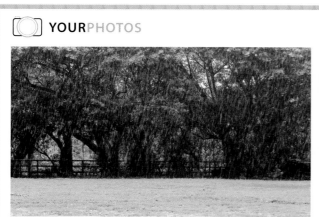

♡ ◯ →

♥ 92 likes

This was on a Thursday afternoon. Usually I have a soccer game on Thursdays, but there wasn't a game that day because of the rain. I love taking pictures of the rain!

♡ ◯ →

♥ 78 likes

It was cold, and there was a lot of snow, but my kids were very happy because there was no school that day. The snow was fun for them to play in.

♡ ◯ →

♥ 56 likes

This was a great day last summer. It was hot and sunny, and my friends and I were happy because we were all together at the beach. It was my friend Michael's birthday—he was 29!

♡ ◯ →

♥ 112 likes

This was last year. The weather was beautiful, but we were at home because my son was sick. He was so sad!

 GRAMMAR IN CONTEXT Simple past of *be*

Was and *wasn't* (*was not*) are the past forms of *is*, *isn't*, and *am not*.

Were and *weren't* (*were not*) are the past forms of *are* and *aren't*.

I wasn't happy because it was cold.
My kids were very happy!

See Grammar focus on page 165.

4 IDENTIFY Find all the examples of the simple past of *be* in the photo descriptions.

5 INTEGRATE Answer the questions with the correct past tense form of *be* and information from the photo descriptions.

1   In photo 1, what was the weather like?   _There was a lot of rain. The weather was bad._

2   In photo 2, why weren't the kids at school?   _____

3   In photo 3, where were the photographer and his friends?   _____

4   Why were they happy?   _____

5   In photo 4, why was the little boy at home?   _____

6   What was the weather like?   _____

6 WHAT'S YOUR ANGLE? Find two of your photos or think of an event in your life where the weather was important. Where were you? What was the weather like that day?

I was in Finland. It was very cold.

> **WRITING SKILL Adding information: Using *because***
>
> We use *because* to explain why. Linking ideas with *because* makes your writing easier to understand and more interesting.
>
> *My friends and I were so happy because we were all together at the beach.*

7 IDENTIFY Listen. Match the situation to the reason.

1   My sister wasn't at work yesterday.

2   The streets were dangerous yesterday.

3   We were at the beach.

4   The children were at home all day.

5   My roommate wasn't home yesterday.

6   There weren't any people in the park this morning.

a   The weather was cold.

b   There was a lot of snow.

c   She was sick.

d   There was rain.

e   The weather was warm.

f   He was at his parents' house.

8 WHAT'S YOUR ANGLE? Choose the option that is true for you. Then give a reason.

1   I *like / don't like* snow because _____.

2   I *love / hate* hot weather because _____.

3   In my opinion, the weather yesterday *was / wasn't* nice because _____.

4   I *was / wasn't* happy yesterday because _____.

5   We *were / weren't* outside a lot last weekend because _____.

9 WRITE Write 2–3 sentences to describe your photos from Exercise 6. Describe your feelings about the weather and why it was important that day.

10 IMPROVE Read your descriptions.

Did you...

■   use the correct forms of *was(n't)* and *were(n't)*?

■   use the correct words to talk about the weather?

■   use *because* to give reasons?

11 SHARE Switch photos and descriptions with a partner. Check his or her work and ask him or her a question about each photo.

Who was with you in this photo? Why were you there?

7.2 Famous Firsts

1 **ACTIVATE** Look at the calendar. Discuss with the class.

1 What month is it now?

2 When are some important days or famous holidays?

3 What is the weather like in each month?

January 31 Days	Febuary 28 Days	March 31 Days	April 30 Days	May 31 Days	June 30 Days
July 31 Days	August 31 Days	September 30 Days	October 31 Days	November 30 Days	December 31 Days

VOCABULARY DEVELOPMENT Dates

To write dates, we use the month + the day + the year.

4/18/1988 = April 18, 1988

When we speak, we use ordinal numbers for days. Most ordinal numbers are formed with number + *-th*. Some are irregular.

1st first	*2nd second*	*3rd third*	*4th fourth*	*5th fifth*	*6th sixth*
7th seventh	*8th eighth*	*9th ninth*	*10th tenth*	*11th eleventh*	*12th twelfth*
20th twentieth	*30th thirtieth*	*31st thirty-first*			

Read most years as two numbers:

1620 = sixteen twenty

Other years:

1908 = nineteen oh eight   *2001 = two thousand and one*   *2012 = two thousand and twelve OR twenty twelve*

2 **BUILD** Read the dates out loud. Then listen and check your answers.

1 12/14/1911

2 March 6, 1937

3 9/22/1944

4 July 31, 1492

5 6/12/1959

6 11/18/2012

7 July 24, 1897

8 January 2, 1701

3 **WHAT'S YOUR ANGLE?** Work with a partner. Say three dates that are important to you. Your partner guesses why the dates are important. Switch roles.

A: April eighth, nineteen ninety.

B: Is that your birthday?

READING SKILL Understanding *and* and *but*

We use *and* to connect related ideas.

*Roald Amundsen was the first person to reach the South Pole on December 14, 1911, **and** he was also the first person to reach the North Pole in 1926.*

We use *but* to connect different ideas.

*There weren't many women pilots in the early 20th century, **but** Amelia Earhart and her teacher were both women.*

4 IDENTIFY Read the two sentences. Are they *Related* or *Different*?

1 My cousin is a pilot. She works for British Airways.   (Related) Different
2 I like taking the train. I don't like flying because it's scary.   Related Different
3 Yesterday was cold and rainy. Today is warm and sunny.   Related Different
4 The Wright brothers were the first to fly an airplane in 1903.
   They weren't the first people to have the idea.   Related Different
5 The first men to step on the moon in 1969 were the astronauts
   Neil Armstrong and Buzz Aldrin. Their flight was called Apollo 11.   Related Different
6 Many people were excited about Apollo 11. Some people were
   nervous because it was dangerous.   Related Different

5 INTEGRATE Rewrite the sentences from Exercise 4. Make the two sentences into one sentence using *and* or *but*.

My cousin is a pilot, and she works for British Airways.

6 ASSESS Skim the article. Why were the women famous?

7 IDENTIFY Read the article. Find examples of *and* and *but* and the important dates.

 Women in Flight

*Parachuting

Amelia Earhart

Amelia Earhart was born in Kansas on July 24th, 1897. When Amelia was young, airplanes were still new. She learned to fly in 1921. There weren't many women pilots then, but her teacher, Neta Snook, was a woman.

On May 20, 1932, she flew solo across the Atlantic. People were excited because she was the second person to do this, and she was the first woman to do it!

Amelia wanted to be the first woman to fly around the world, but sadly she wasn't. On July 2, 1937, she and her plane were lost in the Pacific Ocean during the trip.

Valentina Tereshkova

Valentina Tereshkova was born in Russia on March 6, 1937. As a young woman, she was a factory worker, but she was also interested in parachuting*. She applied to be a cosmonaut in 1962, and she was selected partly because she was good at parachuting.

On June 16, 1963, Valentina was the first woman to go into space. Her space flight was Vostok 6. Many people were excited about it because she was a woman and also because her flight was longer than all of the American astronauts' flights. She was in space for 70 hours and four minutes.

—Adapted from *The Oxford Encyclopedia of Women in World History* edited by Bonnie G. Smith

8 IDENTIFY Complete the timeline with the missing data.

Dates	Events
7/24/1897	
	Amelia learns to fly.
	Amelia flies solo across Atlantic.
1937	Valentina is born.
	Valentina applies to be cosmonaut.
6/16/1963	

> **GRAMMAR IN CONTEXT Simple past with *be*: Questions**
>
> We form *yes/no* questions with *be* in the simple past with:
>
> *Was / Were* + subject…?
> *Were Amelia Earhart and Valentina Tereshkova famous? Yes, they were.*
> *Was Amelia Earhart from the United Kingdom? No, she wasn't.*
>
> We form *wh-* questions with *be* in the simple past with:
>
> Question word + *was / were* + subject…?
> *Why **were** they famous?*

See Grammar focus on page 165.

9 INTEGRATE Answer the questions about the article.

1. Where was Amelia Earhart born?
2. Who was her teacher?
3. Where was her plane lost?
4. What was Valentina Tereshkova's job as a young woman?
5. Where was she from?
6. Why were people excited about the Vostok 6 flight?

10 APPLY Look at the texts again. Write two new questions with *was* or *were* about each woman.

11 INTERACT Work with a partner. Ask and answer your questions from Exercise 10.

12 WHAT'S YOUR ANGLE? Find out about a famous person in your country who was the first to do something. Tell the class who the person was and give the important date(s).

PRIME CREW OF FIFTH MANNED APOLLO MISSION
NEIL A. ARMSTRONG   MICHAEL COLLINS   EDWIN E. ALDRIN, JR.

81

7.3 Around the World

1 ACTIVATE Look at the image. Discuss with the class.

1 Where are the people?
2 Who do the volunteers help?
3 What do they teach them about?

Volunteers teach women in Swaziland about business and health

2 WHAT'S YOUR ANGLE? Do you volunteer for, raise money for, or give to a charity? Which charity? Who does it help?

LISTENING SKILL Listening for the beginning and ending of sentences

🔊 Speakers usually pause between sentences, which helps you know when a new sentence starts.

So, was the journey a success? [pause] The journey was a huge success.

A speaker's voice sometimes goes up at the end of a question.

So, was the journey a success?

It usually goes down at the end of a statement.

The journey was a huge success.

Speakers also pause when there is a comma. Make sure you listen for a complete thought.

He didn't travel by car, [pause] van, [pause] or bus.

3 🔊 NOTICE Listen to the pairs of sentences. Choose the word that begins the *second* sentence.

1	travel	plane	train	we	traveled	boat
2	how	weather	Australia	it	was	hot
3	were	nice	people	they	really	friendly
4	raised	charity	money	how	they	have
5	traveled	China	Laos	Thailand	finally	London

4 ▶ IDENTIFY Watch the video. Complete the statements.

1 Steve and his friends traveled around the world in a
_____.

2 Steve did this because he wanted to _____.

3 The name of the charity was _____.

4 They first traveled across Europe from London to
_____.

5 After New Zealand, they traveled to _____.

6 They returned to Europe by _____.

GRAMMAR IN CONTEXT Simple past: Regular verbs

We add *-ed* to form the simple past of most regular verbs. The form of the simple past is the same for every subject (*I, you, he,* etc.).

*We **worked** for Oxfam in 2008.*
*He **raised** money for charity.*
*They **planned** for their trip.*
*I **studied** business at the university.*

See Grammar focus on page 165.

5 ▶ **INTEGRATE** Watch the video again. Complete the summary with the past tense of the correct verbs.

appear	call	want	plan	use	travel	return	raise	visit	start

Steve Moore ¹_____to raise money for charity, so he and his friends ²_____ a very special journey. They ³_____ it "Follow That Fire Engine."

They ⁴_____ the journey in London in 2011. They ⁵_____ a large red fire engine called Martha. They ⁶_____ across five continents and ⁷_____ 28 countries. From the United States, they ⁸_____ to Europe by boat. After the trip, they ⁹_____ on TV. They ¹⁰_____ £120,000 for charity.

6 **WHAT'S YOUR ANGLE?** What do you think about Steve's charity trip? Was it a good idea? Why?

PRONUNCIATION SKILL Simple past endings /t/, /d/, /id/

The *-ed* ending on past tense regular verbs sounds different in different words.

In words ending in *t* or *d*, the *-ed* ending sounds like /id/. It adds a syllable.
started   ended

In words ending in *ch, f, k, p, ss, sh,* or *x*, the *-ed* ending sounds like /t/. It does not add a syllable.
worked   passed   watched   fixed

In other words, the ending sounds like /d/. It does not add a syllable.
called   stayed   raised

7 ◀» **NOTICE** Listen. Write *1* for one syllable or *2* for two syllables.

1	acted	_____	5	washed	_____
2	showed	_____	6	stopped	_____
3	painted	_____	7	added	_____
4	played	_____	8	checked	_____

8 ◀» **APPLY** Choose the correct pronunciation of *-ed*. Then listen and repeat.

1	started	/id/	/t/	/d/	6	watched	/id/	/t/	/d/
2	ended	/id/	/t/	/d/	7	fixed	/id/	/t/	/d/
3	worked	/id/	/t/	/d/	8	called	/id/	/t/	/d/
4	passed	/id/	/t/	/d/	9	stayed	/id/	/t/	/d/
5	washed	/id/	/t/	/d/	10	raised	/id/	/t/	/d/

9 **WHAT'S YOUR ANGLE?** When was the last time you helped someone? Tell a partner. Who was it? What did you do?

7.4 Oops! My Mistake!

1 **ACTIVATE** Look at the pictures. What do you think happened? How do the people feel?

REAL-WORLD ENGLISH Apologizing

When we apologize for something small (not very important), we can keep it simple.

Oops, sorry!   *Sorry I'm late!*
Sorry about that!   *My mistake!*

When we apologize for something big (important), we add more feeling and more explanation.

I'm (really / very / so) sorry for (being rude / not calling you).
I (missed your calls / wasn't at the meeting) yesterday. I was (very busy / sick).
I'm so late! It's because I missed the first train and the second train was late.

To accept an apology, we often use phrases such as:

It's / That's OK.
Don't worry (about it).
(It's) No problem.

2 ANALYZE Decide if each mistake is big or small.

1 You're 30 minutes late to dinner with a friend. _____

2 You called the wrong number on the phone. _____

3 You spilled some water at the restaurant. _____

4 You're five minutes late to class. _____

5 You missed your grandmother's 80th birthday party. _____

6 You were in a bad mood and not nice to your roommate. _____

3 INTERACT Work with a partner. Look at the Real-World English box. What language would you use in each situation from Exercise 2?

4 ▶ IDENTIFY Watch the video. Listen for Andy's four apologies.

5 ▶ INTEGRATE Answer the questions.

1 The first thing Andy apologizes for in Scene 1 is _____.
   a not cleaning the kitchen
   b not taking out the trash
   c not sharing his food with Max

2 His reason is that _____.
   a he wasn't home
   b he was sick
   c he was tired

3 Next, Andy apologizes for _____ on the floor.
   a the clothes
   b the school papers
   c the tissues

4 His excuse was that he isn't _____.
   a good at basketball
   b good at cleaning
   c a good roommate

5 In Scene 2, Andy and Max *both* apologize to Professor Lopez for _____.
   a being late
   b missing class
   c spilling tea

6 After Andy spills his tea, Professor Lopez responds by saying, _____.
   a "Oh no!"
   b "That's OK, Andy."
   c "Don't worry, guys."

6 ANALYZE Think about the things Andy apologizes for. Are any of them big, important things? Explain.

7 INTERACT Work with a partner. Brainstorm 2–3 situations in which you might need to apologize. Then choose one and write a conversation.

8 SHARE Work with another pair. Act out your role play from Exercise 7. Was it a small mistake or a big mistake? Did you use the right language to apologize?

GO ONLINE
to create your own version
of the English For Real video.

85

7.5 Excuses, Excuses!

1 🔊 **ACTIVATE** Listen to the conversations. Match them to the pictures.

a _____ b _____ c _____ d _____

2 🔊 **IDENTITY** Put the reasons and excuses in the correct place in the table for each conversation from Exercise 1. Listen again and check.

Reasons for apology	can't help with essay	missed phone call	can't go to party	missed class
Excuses	phone wasn't on	works on that day	was with grandmother	is tired

Conversation	Reason for apology	Excuse
a		
b		
c		
d		

3 **WHAT'S YOUR ANGLE?** Were you ever in a situation like the ones from Exercise 1? Describe what happened.

My friend asked for help with a job application, but I was very busy.

> **SPEAKING Making excuses**
>
> When we miss something important or we can't help someone, we can use phrases with *sorry* and give a reason.
>
> *I'm really sorry for not helping you yesterday. I was very busy.*
> *Sorry, I can't go to the movies with you tonight. I have a big test tomorrow.*
> *I missed your party because I was sick. Sorry about that!*

4 **INTEGRATE** Work with a partner. Read each scenario. Does Student A or Student B need to make an excuse? Choose one scenario and write the conversation.

Student A	Student B
1 You moved last weekend. You needed help.	You were in California for work last weekend.
2 You were sick yesterday.	You invited your friend for dinner yesterday.
3 You need a ride to the airport tomorrow.	You have classes all day.
4 The weather was beautiful on Sunday. You were in the park.	You visited Student A on Sunday. He or she wasn't home.

5 **INTERACT** Role-play your scenario from Exercise 4 with your partner. Then choose another scenario and switch roles so you each make an excuse.

8 History

UNIT SNAPSHOT

What kind of place is the Ritz Hotel? 88
What are *platform shoes*? 93
Who ran the first four-minute mile? 98

▼ What can we learn about the past from places like this?

▼ How do you learn about history?

▼ Talk about an historic place in your country.

BEHIND THE PHOTO

REAL-WORLD GOAL

Write an online review for an historic place in your country

Take the history quiz to see what you know. Compare your answers with a partner.

1 When was the first English dictionary published?
   a 1515   b 1604   c 1776   d 1859

2 When was the first cell phone call made?
   a 1943   b 1973   c 1983   d 1993

3 What was the nickname of the Englishman Edward Teach, born in 1680?
   a Banksy the artist   b Grock the clown   c Blackbeard the pirate

4 What was Florence Foster Jenkins known for? She was _____
   a a great nurse.   b a terrible singer.   c an important scientist.

8.1 A Ritzy Business

1 ACTIVATE Think of a famous building in your city or country. What is it famous for? How old is it? Share with the class.

Burj Al Arab, Dubai

The Great Wall of China

The Taj Mahal, India

GRAMMAR IN CONTEXT Simple past of irregular verbs

With irregular verbs, we do not add -ed for the simple past form. There are no rules. They all have different forms.

begin → began	lose → lost
buy → bought	make → made
do → did	see → saw
get → got	spend → spent
go → went	take → took
have → had	think → thought
know → knew	write → wrote

See Grammar focus on page 166.

2 WHAT'S YOUR ANGLE? Using three irregular verbs, describe an interesting building you know.

Last year, I saw an interesting old building in Spain, the Alhambra. It got its name from the Arabic word for "red." I thought it was beautiful. I took many photos of it.

LISTENING SKILL Use visuals to help you understand

When you listen to a lecture, podcast, or video, the accompanying images can help you understand context. Look for images of people and places as you listen. The images can also help you understand new vocabulary.

3 ASSESS Look at the images related to a history podcast. What do they tell you about the topic? Discuss your ideas with a partner.

I think this is a podcast about the Ritz Hotel.

BUILDING HISTORY

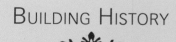

Learn about the history of famous buildings from all over the world!

4 🔊 **APPLY** Listen to the podcast. Use the visuals to help you understand.

5 🔊 **IDENTIFY** Choose the correct answers. Then listen again and check.

1 Cesar Ritz was from _____.
   a France   b Switzerland   c England

2 He opened the Ritz Hotel in London in _____.
   a 1806   b 1898   c 1906

3 He wanted the hotel to look like a building in _____.
   a Paris   b Switzerland   c London

4 The hotel _____ in its first two years.
   a made a lot of money   b lost money   c was a big success

5 The word *ritzy* means _____.
   a very popular   b beautiful and expensive   c French

6 People can spend _____ on a room at the Ritz.
   a £40   b £400–4,000   c £400,000

6 **INTEGRATE** Complete the sentences using the past tense form of the correct verbs.

spend	get	know	begin	lose	go

1 The hotel _____ its name from its first owner.
2 Cesar Ritz _____ time working in restaurants and hotels.
3 In its first two years, the hotel _____ money.
4 In the 1920s and 1930s, many rich and famous people _____ there.
5 Everyone _____ the Ritz Hotel!
6 People _____ to use the word *ritzy*.

> **ⓠ** **VOCABULARY DEVELOPMENT Time expressions**
>
> To talk about the past, we can use *last* + noun and noun + *ago*.
>
> ***last*** *night / week / month / year*
> _____ *days / weeks / months / years* ***ago***
>
> We can use *on* and *in* to talk about a specific date.
>
> ***on*** *Monday*   *on August 15*
> ***in*** *January*   *in 1989*
>
> We can use *in the* + time to talk about a longer period of time.
>
> ***in the*** *(early / late) 1800s / 1980s*

7 **USE** Choose the correct time expressions to complete the text about the history of hotels in England.

Hundreds of years ¹*ago / last*, most travelers rented rooms or stayed at inns, which were small, family-owned hotels. Big hotels, like the ones we have today, began to open in the ²*1800 / 1800s*, after people started to travel by train. The London and Birmingham railway built the first hotel at a train station ³*in / in the* 1839. A bigger one, the Great Western, opened ⁴*in / on* June 1854. Many more opened in the late ⁵*1800 / 1800s* and early ⁶*1900s / 1900*. These hotels were grand and had beautiful rooms and skilled chefs. But in the ⁷*last / late* 70 years, hotels changed. ⁸*Now / Years ago*, many are plain and useful, not grand and beautiful.

8 **WHAT'S YOUR ANGLE?** Think about a hotel stay you had that was really great or really bad. When did you stay there? What was so great or so bad about it?

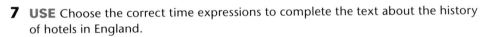

Ten years ago, I stayed at a great hotel in Mexico. It was near the beach, and the people there were friendly. It wasn't expensive, but the rooms were clean and interesting. They had lots of art, plants, and bright colors. I only spent $20 per night!

9 **INTERACT** Share your story with a partner. Did you have a similar experience?

1 ACTIVATE Read Gilberto's timeline.

1 Where is he from?
2 Where does he live now?
3 What is his job?

1980 was born, grew up in Portugal

1994 began high school

1998 went to college

2002 finished college, got a job at a bank

2005 left job

2005–2008 studied photography

2010 left home, came to the United States

2012 met my future wife

2014 got married

2015 had first child

2 WHAT'S YOUR ANGLE? Create your own timeline. Include important events from your life.

3 INTERACT Work with a partner. Do you have similar timelines?

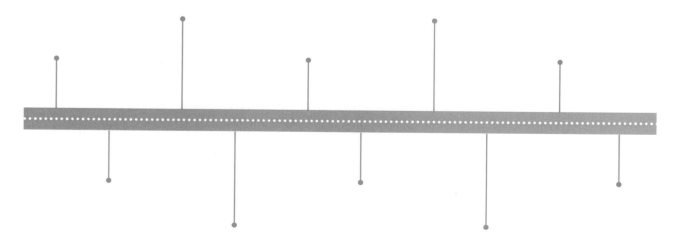

4 IDENTIFY Now read Gilberto's bio. Find three details from the bio that weren't in the timeline.

Gilberto Mendes

I was born in a small town near Lisbon in 1980, and I grew up in Portugal with my parents and grandparents. I didn't have brothers or sisters. I began high school in 1994 and finished in 1998. After that, I went to the University of Lisbon. I finished college in 2002, and then I got a job at a bank. I made good money, but I didn't like it. It was boring. I didn't feel happy there.

In 2005, I left my job at the bank and started to study photography. Next, I decided to come to the United States and look for a job. I didn't know anyone here, and I didn't speak English, but that didn't stop me. I came, and I got a job at a small photography studio. After that, I began to learn English, and I also met a nice woman named Lisa. She didn't work at the studio, but she was also a photographer. Later, in 2014, Lisa and I got married. One year later, we had our first child.

 GRAMMAR IN CONTEXT Simple past: Negative

We form the simple past negative with *didn't*: Subject (*I, you, he*, etc.) + *didn't* + verb.

I **didn't have** brothers or sisters.

We form the negative in the same way for both regular and irregular verbs.

I **didn't play** baseball. (NOT ~~I didn't played baseball.~~)
I **didn't speak** English. (NOT ~~I didn't spoke English.~~)

See Grammar focus on page 166.

5 IDENTIFY Read Gilberto's bio again. Find the positive past tense verbs. Find the negative past tense verbs.

6 INTEGRATE Listen and write the verb in each sentence.

1 I _____ college in 2004.
2 I _____ my studies.
3 I _____ to work at a big company.
4 I quickly _____ to play guitar.
5 I _____ some cool songs.
6 My parents _____ my music.

7 WHAT'S YOUR ANGLE? Think about when you were a child. Write a true sentence about yourself as a child for each verb in the simple past positive and the simple past negative.

1 grow up   *I grew up in Indonesia. I didn't grow up in Australia.*
2 live   _____
3 like   _____
4 have   _____
5 know   _____
6 speak   _____
7 [choose your own verb] _____

91

To make our writing better, we can use sequence words like *then, next, after that*, and *later* to connect events. Sequence words show us the order of events.

I finished high school in 1998. **After that**, *I went to the University of Lisbon.*
I finished college in 2002, and **then** *I got a job at a bank.*
Next, *I decided to come to the United States and look for a job here.*
Later, *in 2014, Lisa and I got married.* **One year later**, *we had our first child.*

8 **USE** Rewrite the sentences. Add sequence words.

| next | later | one month later | two years later | then | after that |

1 Layla was born in Iraq in 1979. Her parents took her to the United Arab Emirates in 1980.
   Layla was born in Iraq in 1979. One year later, her parents took her to the United Arab Emirates.

2 They lived in Germany for five years. They moved to France.
   They lived in Germany for five years, and then they moved to France.

3 They got married in 2002. Their daughter was born in 2004.

4 Vinit moved to London. He started college.

5 We arrived here in August. We began classes in September.

6 Jeannie studied business in college. She opened a small business.

7 She took piano lessons. She decided to take singing lessons.

8 I traveled around South America for six months. I came home and got a job.

9 **WRITE** Write your biography. Use your timeline and Gilberto's bio to help you. Include sequence words and positive and negative past tense verbs.

10 **IMPROVE** Read your bio. Fix errors and check for information you learned.

Did you...
■ use the correct positive and negative past tense verb forms?
■ use sequence words to make your writing better?
■ use *because* to give reasons?
■ use capital letters correctly?

11 **SHARE** Switch bios with a classmate. Check each other's work.

8.3 They Wore That?

1 VOCABULARY Look at the pictures in the article. Label the clothes.

a shirt	a pair of shoes	a pair of pants	a pair of jeans	a hat
a jacket	a dress	a skirt	a **T-shirt**	

⚷ Oxford 3000™

2 WHAT'S YOUR ANGLE? What clothes do your classmates have on today? Try to find one example of each item. What colors are they?

3 ASSESS Read the article and look at the pictures. Whose clothes changed more over time, women's clothes or men's clothes? Why do you think so?

Did they **Really** Wear That?

Fashions change fast. Look at the clothes people in the United States wore!

Q: What clothes were popular in the 1950s?

A: In the 1950s, big skirts were popular, and many women wore hats. Some young men liked to wear a white T-shirt, a motorcycle jacket, and blue jeans.

Q: Did women wear jeans, too?

A: Not really. At work and at school, women wore dresses and skirts, not pants or jeans.

Q: What did people wear in the 1960s?

A: In the 1960s, we saw "baby doll" dresses on women. We also saw tie-dyed shirts and bell-bottom jeans—on men and women.

Q: Did styles change in the 1970s?

A: We had some crazy clothes in the 1970s! Maxi dresses were popular with women. There were a lot of interesting patterns. Some men wore unusual shirts or pants, and platform shoes were hot!

Q: How did we dress in the 1980s?

A: In the 1980s, people wore bright colors. A popular style for women was a big, long shirt and tight pants. Acid-washed jeans and jean jackets were also very popular.

Q: Did we look different in the 1990s?

A: In the 1990s, the "grunge look" was in. A lot of people—men and women—wore big, baggy pants and flannel shirts.

1	_____
2	_____
3	_____
4	_____
5	_____
6	_____
7	_____
8	_____
9	_____

READING SKILL Scanning for specific information

When you scan a text, you don't read all of it. You look for key words to find information you want to know.

4 IDENTIFY Scan the article. Choose the correct decade for each style.

	1950s	1960s	1970s	1980s	1990s
1 maxi dresses, platform shoes	☐	☐	☐	☐	☐
2 "grunge," flannel shirts	☐	☐	☐	☐	☐
3 big skirts and hats for women	☐	☐	☐	☐	☐
4 bright colors, acid-washed jeans, and jean jackets	☐	☐	☐	☐	☐
5 bell-bottom jeans	☐	☐	☐	☐	☐

5 WHAT'S YOUR ANGLE? Choose your favorite clothes from the article. Tell a partner. Why do you like them? Do you wear similar clothes now?

I like the 1950s clothes. I have a jacket like that, and I wore it yesterday.

GRAMMAR IN CONTEXT Simple past: *Yes/no* questions

We form simple past *yes/no* questions with: *Did* + subject + verb? The form is the same for every subject (*I, you, he*, etc.).

***Did** they really **wear** that?*

In short answers, we use *did* and *didn't*. We don't use the main verb.

***Did** women **wear** pants? No, they **didn't**.*
***Did** styles **change** in the 1970s? Yes, they **did**.*

See Grammar focus on page 166.

6 🔊 **INTEGRATE** Listen to questions about the article. Choose the correct answers. Compare with a partner.

1 Yes, they were.	No, they weren't.	Yes, they did.	No, they didn't.
2 Yes, they were.	No, they weren't.	Yes, they did.	No, they didn't.
3 Yes, they were.	No, they weren't.	Yes, they did.	No, they didn't.
4 Yes, they were.	No, they weren't.	Yes, they did.	No, they didn't.
5 Yes, they were.	No, they weren't.	Yes, they did.	No, they didn't.
6 Yes, they were.	No, they weren't.	Yes, they did.	No, they didn't.

7 🔊 **IMPROVE** Listen again and check your answers.

8 INTERACT Did people wear the same clothes in your country? Whose clothes changed more, people's in the United States or in your country? Make notes and then discuss with a partner.

Did men wear bell-bottom jeans in the 1970s in your country?

9 **WHAT'S YOUR ANGLE?** Think about the clothes you wore when you were a child and when you were a teenager. Make notes.

I often wore jeans and T-shirts when I was a child.

10 **INTERACT** Work with a partner. Ask questions. Did you wear similar clothes when you were younger?

Student A: Did you wear jeans a lot?

Student B: No, I wore dresses and skirts, but I always wore jeans when I was a teenager. Now, I usually wear jeans on the weekend.

A young fashion designer shops at Soweto's Maponya Mall in Johannesburg, South Africa

1 ACTIVATE Look at the pictures from the video.

1   What kind of news do you think Max, Andy, and Kevin got in each picture?

2   How do they feel? Why do you think so?

2 ▶ **ASSESS** Watch the video. Then look at the pictures again.

1   What news did Andy give Max just before picture 1?
    a   He passed his big test.
    b   He got a new job.

2   How did Max react?
    a   He was happy for Andy.
    b   He felt bad about his own grades.

3   What news did Andy give Max just before picture 2?
    a   He got tickets to go home for winter break.
    b   He decided to stay at the apartment for winter break.

4   What did Max say? How did he *really* feel?
    a   He said, "That's cool" but felt a little bad.
    b   He said, "That's cool" and felt excited for Andy and Kevin.

5   What news did Max give Andy and Kevin just before picture 3?
    a   He can't go home because it's too expensive.
    b   He doesn't want to go home.

6   How did Andy react?
    a   He said, "That's too bad."
    b   He said, "I'm sorry!"

7   What was Max's good news?
    a   He won a plane ticket for next winter.
    b   He won a free pass to the art museum.

8   What do Kevin and Andy say (picture 4)?
    a   "That's great!"
    b   "Congratulations!"

ENGLISH FOR REAL

When someone gives you news, give a reaction that fits the situation.

I passed my test!	*Wow! That's great! / (That's) Cool! / Congratulations!*
Today's my birthday.	*Happy birthday!*
I didn't pass the test.	*Oh. I'm sorry! / That's too bad.*
I lost my wallet!	*Oh no!*

The tone of your voice should match the situation, too. For example, if the news is very exciting, sound very excited.

3 IDENTIFY Match the situations with an appropriate response. What should you say to your friend?

Your friend…

1 has a great new job.
2 lost her house keys.
3 bought a new car.
4 is getting married.
5 lost his job.

You say:

a That's too bad.
b Wow, that is amazing news! Congratulations!
c That's cool!
d Oh no, that's terrible! I'm sorry to hear that.
e Wow, that's great!

4 ANALYZE Compare your answers in Exercise 3 with a partner.

1 Why did you choose them?
2 How would your tone of voice change in each situation?
3 Are these reactions the same in your language?

5 INTERACT Work with a partner. Practice reacting to different kinds of news.

I got a new job. It pays well.
Wow, that's great!

Student A

1 You got a new job. It pays well.
2 You bought a house.
3 Your friend is in the hospital.
4 You lost your new phone.
5 It's your birthday.
6 You spilled coffee on your new white shirt.

Student B

1 Your sister had a baby today.
2 You lost your job.
3 You missed your bus. The next one is in an hour.
4 You won a trip to Hawaii.
5 You met a famous person you love.
6 You ordered food from a restaurant, and it was bad.

6 ANALYZE Work with another group. Discuss your role plays.

1 Which situations in Exercise 5 were serious or exciting?
2 Which situations were not very serious or exciting?
3 How did your tone of voice change to match the situation?

GO ONLINE
to create your own version
of the English For Real video.

8.5 Making History

1 **ACTIVATE** What do you know about the four-minute mile? Guess the correct options, and then listen to the presentation and check.

1 Before 1954, a runner from *Sweden / England / Switzerland* held the world record for running one mile.

2 People didn't think it was *possible / difficult / interesting* to run a mile in under four minutes.

3 In 1954, Roger Bannister ran a mile in *4 minutes and one second / 3 minutes, 59.4 seconds / 3 minutes, 55 seconds*.

4 In *1979 / 1989 / 1999*, someone broke Roger Bannister's record.

5 The runner who broke the record, Hicham El Guerrouj, was from *Algeria / Morocco / Tunisia*.

—Adapted from *A Dictionary of Sports Studies* (1st ed.) by Alan Tomlinson

Hicham El Guerrouj

PRONUNCIATION SKILL Rising and falling intonation in statements

When we speak, the pitch of our voices go up and down. It often goes up and down on the most important word or words in a statement. Often, it goes up then down on the last word.

Many people thought it wasn't possible.

2 **NOTICE** Listen. Select the words where you hear the pitch rise. Then listen again and repeat.

1 (Many) people thought it wasn't (possible.)

2 He held this record for nine years.

3 Roger Bannister broke the record.

4 He ran a mile in three minutes and fifty-nine seconds.

5 Hicham El Guerrouj set a new record.

6 That's the record to this day.

3 **WHAT'S YOUR ANGLE?** Choose a sports event or other achievement from history you are interested in.

Take notes about:
- what happened.
- when it happened (the important dates).
- the people in the event.
- why it was an exciting event.

SPEAKING Talking about dates

Remember, when you say a date, use ordinal numbers for the days.

July 14th (July fourteenth)

Read most years as two numbers:

1066 (ten sixty-six)   1984 (nineteen eighty-four)   2016 (twenty sixteen)   1808 (eighteen oh eight)

From 2000–2009:

2001 (two thousand and one)

4 **INTERACT** Work with a partner. Practice talking about the events you chose. Use your notes from Exercise 4. Make sure you say the dates correctly and use correct intonation.

5 **SHARE** Share your information with the class.

Now go to page 154 for the Unit 8 Review.

9 Comforts

▼ Where are the two girls?   ▼ What places make you feel happy?   ▼ What people make you feel happy?

BEHIND THE PHOTO

REAL-WORLD GOAL

Order food in a restaurant

1 Complete the sentences about you.

1 My friends and I are happy when _____.

2 Two activities that make me feel happy are _____ and _____.

3 My favorite place is _____ because _____.

4 My favorite day of the week is _____ because

   _____.

5 I feel good when the weather is _____.

6 When I travel, I like to go to _____.

2 Compare your answers to your classmates'.

1 ACTIVATE Label the food and drinks.

| fruit | fish | tea | coffee | meat | rice | milk | vegetables | eggs | bread |

🔑 Oxford 3000™

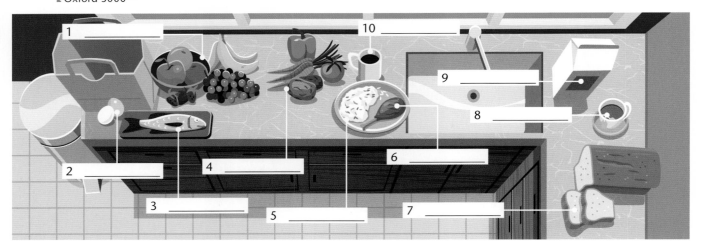

1 _____   10 _____

9 _____

8 _____

2 _____

4 _____

6 _____

3 _____

5 _____   7 _____

2 USE Which food and drink items do you eat or drink? Which *don't* you eat or drink? Write sentences with *every day*, *sometimes*, and *never*.

3 WHAT'S YOUR ANGLE? Imagine you can have only three items from Exercise 1. Which ones do you want? Tell a partner.

I want coffee, milk, and bread. I love coffee with milk in the morning.
I never drink coffee. I want tea, rice, and meat. I eat rice every day.

> **LISTENING SKILL Listening for detail**
>
> You can improve your understanding by listening to a video or piece of audio more than once. The first time you listen, try to get the general idea. The second time you listen, focus on the details.

4 ▶ ASSESS Watch the video once to get the main ideas. Complete the sentences.

1 Jean likes to shop at _____.
2 She likes it because _____.
3 She wants to make _____ for dinner.

5 ▶ IDENTIFY Watch the video a second time. Listen for details. Choose all the correct answers.

1 Which days is the farmers' market open? Choose three.

| Sundays | Tuesdays | Thursdays | Saturdays |
| Mondays | Wednesdays | Fridays | |

2 What does Jean buy at the market for her dinner? Choose seven.

meat	tomatoes	tea	pasta
eggs	garlic	cheese	mushrooms
an onion	bread	rice	cakes

6 ▶ **ASSESS** Watch the video again. Are the statements *True* or *False*?

1	Jean is a babysitter.	True	False
2	Jean goes to the market only on Fridays.	True	False
3	Jean likes cooking.	True	False
4	The farmers at the market come from all over the country.	True	False
5	Jean gets honey for her tea there.	True	False
6	The cheese stand is Jean's favorite because there are so many kinds.	True	False

7 **WHAT'S YOUR ANGLE?** What do you like to cook? Write sentences about the food and what you need to make it. Use a dictionary if you need to. Share with a partner.

I love cooking omelets. To make them, I need some eggs, some cheese, some vegetables, and some olive oil.

GRAMMAR IN CONTEXT Countable and uncountable nouns

Countable nouns can be singular or plural.

an egg   two eggs

Uncountable nouns only have a singular form.

bread   milk

We don't use numbers with uncountable nouns. We can use *some* + uncountable noun in positive sentences. We can use *any* + uncountable nouns in negative sentences.

*Jean buys **some** pasta.   She doesn't have **any** bread.*

We can also use *some* and *any* with plural countable nouns.

*She bought **some** vegetables at the farmers' market.   She didn't buy **any** eggs.*

See Grammar focus on page 167.

8 **IDENTIFY** Choose the correct word.

1   Jean buys *some / any* vegetables.
2   They don't have *some / any* milk.
3   Jean likes to put *a / some* honey in her tea.

4   She wants to eat *an / some* apple.
5   She buys *one / some* bread.
6   She doesn't need *some / any* eggs.

9 **INTEGRATE** You and your roommate are inviting friends for breakfast tomorrow. Student A makes a list. Student B checks the kitchen. Ask and answer questions about what you have in the kitchen.

Student A			Student B		
You need:			**You have:**		
bread	milk	coffee	milk	vegetables	two eggs
fruit	eggs	cheese	apples	tea	rice

A: Do we have any bread?
B: No, but we have some rice.

10 **INTERACT** Read the text and look at the image. Discuss with the class. What are comfort foods for you?

 Comfort Food

Comfort food is food that makes you feel good and happy, often because it reminds you of home cooking or of the time when you were a child.

—Adapted from *The Oxford Encyclopedia of Food and Drink in America*, 2ⁿᵈ ed., edited by Andrew F. Smith

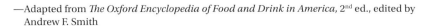

101

9.2 Let's Go Glamping!

1 ACTIVATE What kind of vacations do you like? Look at the images from the text. Is camping a good vacation for you? Tell a partner.

> **READING SKILL Understanding the organization of a text: Topic sentences**
>
> A topic sentence tells you what a paragraph or text is about. The topic sentence is often the first sentence of a paragraph.

2 IDENTIFY Before you read, scan through the text and look for the topic sentences. Which paragraph is about…

1 _____ how expensive glamping is
2 _____ camping in a tent
3 _____ people who prefer glamping, not camping
4 _____ different types of glamping

| Home | About | | Search | 🔍 |

Goodbye, Camping… Hello, Glamping!

A lot of people enjoy camping. They like being outdoors. They sleep in a tent on the ground with no furniture and not much comfort—especially when the weather is wet!

But camping isn't for everyone. Some people think it's uncomfortable. They want to enjoy nature *and* the comfort of a soft bed in a dry room. They don't want to be uncomfortable on their vacation. Say hello to *glamping*!

Glamping = glamorous + camping. There are many different kinds of glamping. You can stay in a comfortable tent, a treehouse high up in the trees, or a cabin next to a lake. Some glamping tents have a lot of the same furniture that a house has!

Of course, comfort costs money. Traditional camping is cheap—often $10 to $30 per night—but glamping can be very expensive. How much does it cost? Well…some places are more expensive than others. One treehouse in South Africa costs only $87 per night, but one glamping hotel in Ecuador costs $1,296 per night!

Traditional tent camping

Treehouse glamping

Tent glamping

3 ASSESS Choose the correct answer.

	Camping	Glamping	Both
1 It's fun.	☐	☐	☐
2 It's for people who enjoy nature.	☐	☐	☐
3 You can sleep in a tree.	☐	☐	☐
4 You sleep in a tent outside.	☐	☐	☐
5 It's similar to a hotel but in nature.	☐	☐	☐
6 There's a bed and some other furniture.	☐	☐	☐
7 There isn't much comfort.	☐	☐	☐
8 It's hard work.	☐	☐	☐

4 INTERACT Take a class vote. Which is more interesting to you—camping or glamping? Why?

5 VOCABULARY Label the furniture items.

refrigerator   lamp   bed   sofa   TV   chair   desk   table

⚲ Oxford 3000™

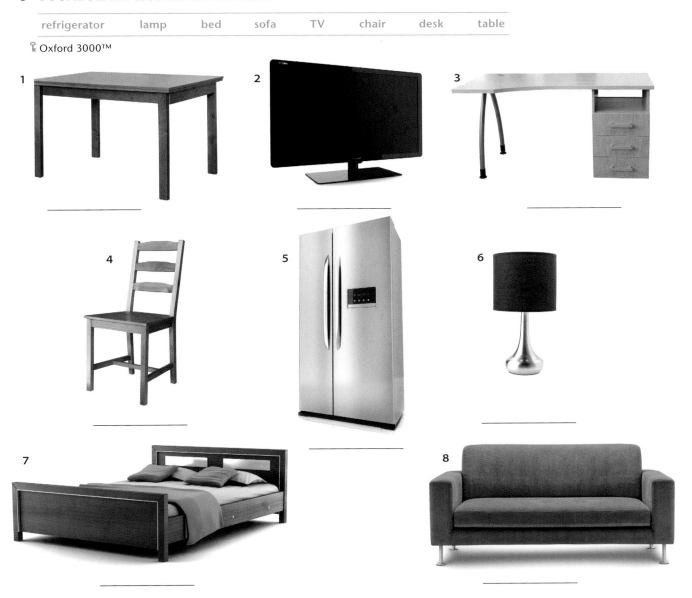

1 _____

2 _____

3 _____

4 _____

5 _____

6 _____

7 _____

8 _____

6 INTERACT Work with a partner. Choose a furniture item and draw a picture of it. Your partner guesses and spells the word. Take turns.

We use *How much…?* to ask about uncountable nouns. We use *How many…?* to ask about countable nouns.

How much furniture does the tent have?   **How many** beds do we need?

We can answer the questions in different ways.

*It doesn't have **any** furniture.*	*We don't need **any** beds.*
***Not much**. It doesn't have **much** furniture.*	***Not many**. We don't need **many** beds.*
*It has **some** furniture.*	*We need **some** beds.*
*It has **a lot of** furniture!*	*We need **a lot of** beds.*

See Grammar focus on page 167.

7 🔊 **INTEGRATE** Complete the sentences with the correct words. Then listen and check.

1   How *much / many* tents are there?   There are *much / a lot of* tents.
2   How *much / many* furniture is there?   There isn't *any / many* furniture.
3   How *much / many* chairs do they have?   They have *some / much* chairs.
4   How *much / many* fun did they have last weekend?   They had *much / a lot of* fun!

8 **ASSESS** Did the people in Exercise 7 go camping or glamping? How do you know?

9 **DEVELOP** Complete the text with the quantifiers.

a lot of	any	much	a lot	some	many

Every year, my family and I go camping. We travel by car and we fill the car with everything we need. Because there isn't ¹_____ space, we pack very carefully. We can't take ²_____ things, but we do take ³_____ food and warm clothes! We don't take ⁴_____ furniture, but we do take ⁵_____ cooking equipment. Camping saves us ⁶_____ of money, but that's not why we do it. We go camping because we love it!

10 **WHAT'S YOUR ANGLE?** Design your perfect vacation space. Is it a camping tent, a glamping tent, or a hotel room? Where is it? What is it like? What furniture does it have? Describe it to a partner.

My perfect vacation space is a camping spot on the beach. It's very quiet. There is no tent, and there are no people.

Ibiza, Balearic islands, Spain

9.3 Welcome to Town!

1 ACTIVATE Think about when you travel to a new city. What are the first things you want to do when you arrive? Tell a partner.

A: The first thing I want to do in a new city is go to my hotel.

B: Really? I want to walk around and see the city.

2 VOCABULARY Which adjectives describe a place? Which describe a person? Which can describe a person or place?

excellent	terrible	all right	hungry	thirsty	tired	ready	open	closed

ℸ Oxford 3000™

place: _____

person: _____

person or place: _____

3 ◀)) **USE** Listen and match the conversations to the images. Then write a short sentence about each situation using the adjectives from Exercise 2.

a _She's ready._

b _____

c _____

d _____

e _____

f _____

g _____

h _____

i _____

105

4 **IDENTIFY** Read the messages between Michael and Manuel. Choose the best summary.

a Manuel is Michael's friend, and Michael suggests a good hotel for him. They arrange to meet that evening.

b Manuel is on a business trip, and Michael suggests a good restaurant. They arrange to meet in the morning.

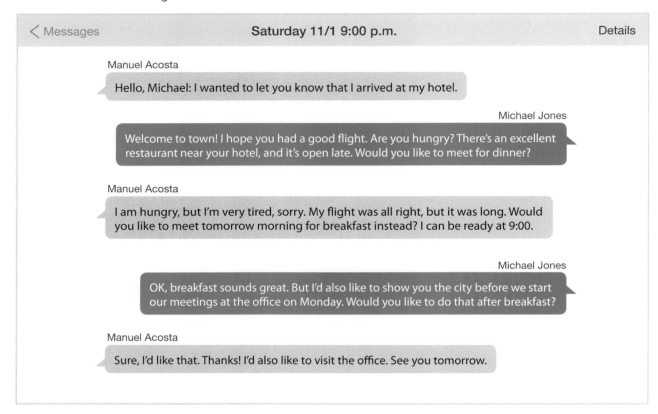

Messages   Saturday 11/1 9:00 p.m.   Details

Manuel Acosta

> Hello, Michael: I wanted to let you know that I arrived at my hotel.

Michael Jones

> Welcome to town! I hope you had a good flight. Are you hungry? There's an excellent restaurant near your hotel, and it's open late. Would you like to meet for dinner?

Manuel Acosta

> I am hungry, but I'm very tired, sorry. My flight was all right, but it was long. Would you like to meet tomorrow morning for breakfast instead? I can be ready at 9:00.

Michael Jones

> OK, breakfast sounds great. But I'd also like to show you the city before we start our meetings at the office on Monday. Would you like to do that after breakfast?

Manuel Acosta

> Sure, I'd like that. Thanks! I'd also like to visit the office. See you tomorrow.

5 **ASSESS** Read the messages again. Are the statements *True* or *False*?

1	Manuel sends his first message from the airport.	True	False
2	Michael offers to go to a restaurant on Saturday night.	True	False
3	Manuel is tired because his flight was terrible.	True	False
4	Michael and Manuel have meetings tomorrow.	True	False
5	Manuel wants to see the city tomorrow.	True	False

> ### GRAMMAR IN CONTEXT *Would like*: Requests and offers
>
> *Would like* is a polite way of saying *want*. We use *Would* + subject + *like* + noun / verb…? to ask what people want.
>
> **Would** you **like** to meet for dinner? *Yes, please. / No, thanks.*
> What **would** you **like** to do today? *I'd like to see the city.*
>
> We use *would like* to ask for something or to say what we want in a polite way. It is the same for every subject. The short form of *would like* is *'d like*.
>
> I**'d like** to visit the office.
> Michael **would like** to show him the city.

See Grammar focus on page 167.

6 **IDENTIFY** Look at the conversation again. Find all the instances of *would like*. Which are requests? Which are offers?

Requests:

Offers:

7 EXPAND Read the statements. Use *would like* to make a request or offer.

1 You need a new laptop for work. (request)
   I'd like a new laptop, please.
2 You're thirsty. (request)
3 You have coffee. Ask your friend. (offer)
4 You want to see the manager. (request)
5 Your friend is having trouble with their computer and you can help. (offer)
6 You want to book a hotel room for two nights. (request)

WRITING SKILL Connecting ideas with *but*

Use *but* to connect two different or opposite ideas. This makes your writing clearer and easier to understand.

*I am hungry, **but** I'm very tired.*
*My flight was all right, **but** it was long.*

8 DEVELOP Choose the logical phrase to complete each sentence.

1 I'd like to go with you to the restaurant now, but _____
   a I'm not ready.
   b I'm very hungry.
2 I'd like to take the bus tour, but _____
   a I bought a ticket.
   b it's expensive.
3 The movie is interesting, but _____
   a I can't see it with you tonight.
   b I think it's boring.
4 I'm at the hotel now, but _____
   a I'd like to go out.
   b the room is very nice.
5 Breakfast is from 7:00 to 9:00, but _____
   a they serve a lot of different foods.
   b I usually get up at 10:00.
6 It's very late, but _____
   a I'm not tired.
   b it's dark outside.

9 WHAT'S YOUR ANGLE? Choose a city you want to visit. What things do you want to see and do? Make a list.

I want to visit Sydney. I want to swim in the sea and climb Sydney Harbour Bridge.

10 PREPARE Work with a partner. Swap your lists from Exercise 9. Imagine you are a tour guide for the city. Make notes on some offers and requests for your partner.

11 WRITE Use paper and pen to "email" the tour guide about your trip. Include two requests. Give your email to your partner so he or she can write back to you.

Hello,

I'm a tourist in Sydney, and I'd like some information about the city. I'd like to climb Sydney Harbour Bridge, but I don't have much money. How much does it cost?

Gabrielle

Hi Gabrielle,

Welcome to Sydney! It costs $70 to climb Sydney Harbour Bridge. Would you like me to book your ticket? It's an excellent place to visit.

Pete

12 WRITE Switch roles. You are the tour guide, and your partner is the visitor.

13 IMPROVE With your partner, check the grammar and spelling in your emails.

Did you…
■ use *would like* to make requests and offers?
■ use *but* to connect ideas that are different?
■ use adjectives to describe places and people?

1 ACTIVATE Is there anything you can't or don't eat? What do you do if you are at a person's house and he or she offers you some?

I don't eat meat. If I am at a person's house and he or she offers me meat, I say, "No, thank you. I'm a vegetarian."

2 ▶ ASSESS Watch the video. What do Max and Andy offer each other?

bubble and squeak

steak and kidney pie

mac and cheese

REAL-WORLD ENGLISH Accepting and rejecting offers

There are various ways to accept an offer.

Polite:	*Would you like some water?*	→	*Yes, please.*
Excited:	*Do you want to try some pie?*	→	*Yes, I'd love to! / I'd love some!*
	Here, have some mac and cheese.	→	*Sure! / OK!*

Say "No, thanks" or "No, thank you" to reject an offer. Give a reason if you can.

	Would you like some pasta?	→	*No, thank you. I ate. / I'm not hungry. / I don't usually eat pasta.*
Don't say	*Would you like some pasta?*	→	*Not really. / No.*

Note: You don't need to give a reason in a restaurant, only with friends or people you know.

3 **IDENTIFY** What phrases do Max and Andy use to reject or accept the offers?

4 **ANALYZE** Read the conversations. Decide if person B's response is appropriate or not appropriate. Give an appropriate response where needed.

1   A: Would you like some fish and rice?
    B: Not really.

2   A: I made some Vietnamese noodle soup. Would you like to try it?
    B: Sure. Thanks!

3   A: Do you want to try some of these tacos?
    B: I'd love to!

4   A: Here, have some of this mushroom pizza.
    B: No. I hate mushrooms!

5   A: This sandwich is really big. Do you want to eat some of it?
    B: No, thanks. I ate lunch a few minutes ago.

6   A: Excuse me, sir. Would you like some more water?
    B: No, thank you.

5 **INTERACT** Discuss your answers in Exercise 4 with a partner. Are the responses the same in your country?

6 **WHAT'S YOUR ANGLE?** Think of your favorite dish or a special dish from your country. Describe it. What is in it?

7 **INTERACT** Work with a partner. Role-play accepting and rejecting offers. Then switch roles.

Student A: Offer Student B some of your favorite dish.

Student B: Reject the offer politely.

Student A: Describe the food and offer again.

Student B: Accept the offer.

GO ONLINE
to create your own version
of the English For Real video.

1 **ACTIVATE** Look at the image and the menu. Where are the people? What do you think they say?

> ### SPEAKING Ordering food and drink
>
> When you order food and drink, it's polite to use the word *please* and to use *would like* / *'d like* instead of *want*.
>
> *I'd like some water, please.* / *Can I have some water? ~~I want water!~~*
>
> When you accept an offer, use *please* or *thanks* / *thank you*.
>
> Q: *Would you like some more coffee?*   A: *Yes, thank you!*

2 **IDENTIFY** Listen to the conversation. Complete the sentences.

1 First, the server asks if they want _____
   a some water   b to order   c some drinks

2 They order some _____ to drink.
   a coffee   b tea   c soda

3 The server asks them if they want _____ with that.
   a milk   b cake   c food

4 Customer 1 orders some ice cream, and customer 2 orders _____.
   a a cookie   b some cookies   c some cake

> ### PRONUNCIATION SKILL Rising tone in polite requests and offers
>
> When using *would like* to offer something, our voice rises at the end.
>
> *Would you like some milk with that?*
>
> When we make a request in the form of a question, our voice also rises at the end.
>
> *Can I have a cookie, please?*
>
> When we make a request using *I'd like*, our voice falls, not rises.
>
> *I'd like some ice cream.*

3 **NOTICE** Listen. Choose the word where the tone rises.

1 Can I get a menu, (please?)
2 Would you like any drinks?
3 I'd like some tea, please.
4 Can I have some milk with that?
5 We'd like some cake, please.
6 Would you like anything else?

4 **USE** Listen again and repeat.

5 **INTEGRATE** Look at the menu. What would you like to order? How would you ask for it?

6 **INTERACT** Work with a partner. Student A is a server at a coffee shop. Student B is a customer. Role-play the situation. Switch roles.

MENU

DRINKS

COFFEE	$2.25
TEA	$2.00
FRUIT SODA	$2.50
HOT CHOCOLATE	$2.50

TREATS

CAKE	$3.00
COOKIES	$2.50
ICE CREAM	$2.50

10 Adventure

What is an adventure?

What is a good place for an adventure?

What do you need for an adventure?

BEHIND THE PHOTO

REAL-WORLD GOAL

Find an "adventure" you can have in your town or city

Can you match these famous places to their locations? Are they good places for an adventure? Put them in order from 1–7, and then compare your answers with a partner.

1	the Andes Mountains _____	a China and Mongolia
2	Versailles Gardens _____	b the United States
3	the Gobi Desert _____	c Australia
4	the Black Forest _____	d South America
5	Lake Victoria _____	e France
6	the Mississippi River _____	f Germany
7	Kakadu National Park _____	g Africa

Top Four Travel Spots

1 ◀)) **ACTIVATE** Label the images. Then listen for the answers.

the **countryside**	the **desert**	the **mountains**	a **garden**	the **forest**
the **sea**	a **lake**	a **village**		

ⵀ Oxford 3000™

1 _____

2 _____

3 _____

4 _____

5 _____

6 _____

7 _____

8 _____

2 ◀)) **IDENTIFY** Listen and number the places from Exercise 1 in the order you hear them.

a countryside _____   c mountains _____   e forest _____   g lake _____

b desert _____   d garden _____   f sea _____   h village _____

3 **WHAT'S YOUR ANGLE?** Think about the places from Exercise 1. Discuss your ideas with a partner.

Which are good places to…?

1 go camping
2 go shopping
3 swim

4 go for a walk
5 have a quiet vacation
6 have an exciting vacation

 LISTENING SKILL Listening for individual words in a sentence

When we speak in a natural way, our words often blend together. Sometimes two or three words can sound like one word.

He lives in a small village. → *He* lɪvzɪnə *small village.*

Look at the tall mountains! → lʊkətðə *tall mountains.*

Listen closely and try to count the words in a sentence. This will help you focus and understand more.

4 ◀)) **IDENTIFY** Listen. How many words are in each sentence?

1 5 / 6 / 7   2 6 / 7 / 8   3 4 / 5 / 6
4 5 / 6 / 7   5 6 / 7 / 8   6 4 / 5 / 6

5 🔊 **DEVELOP** Listen to the sentences from Exercise 4 again. Write the sentences.

We want to tell you about them.

6 🔊 **IDENTIFY** Listen to the travel podcast. Which places do they talk about? Use the vocabulary from Exercise 1.

7 🔊 **INTEGRATE** Listen to the travel podcast again. Are the statements True or False?

1 Pemuteran is in India.	True	False
2 Pemuteran is a village.	True	False
3 The Garden of Cosmic Speculation is in Scotland.	True	False
4 The Garden uses ideas from math and science.	True	False
5 The Adirondack Mountains are in New York City.	True	False
6 There are interesting animals in Madagascar.	True	False

The Garden of Cosmic Speculation

 GRAMMAR IN CONTEXT Object pronouns

We use pronouns in place of nouns. The object pronouns are *me, you, him, her, it, us,* and *them.* Object pronouns go after a verb or a preposition.

We chose our four favorite places to travel this year. Now we want to tell **you** *about* **them***.*

See Grammar focus on page 168.

8 **IDENTIFY** Read the sentences. Choose the words that the object pronoun talks about.

1 Lindsey thinks that Pemuteran is a great place to visit, and I agree with <u>her</u>.
  a Pemuteran   **b Lindsey**   c place

2 Mt. Fuji in Japan is a very popular mountain to climb. Thousands of people climb <u>it</u> every year.
  a Japan   b Mt. Fuji   c people

3 There are so many interesting places in the world. My husband and I want to visit <u>them</u> all!
  a places   b the world   c my husband and I

4 My parents plan to go to Madagascar to see the animals in the rain forest. I want to go with <u>them</u>.
  a the animals   b my parents   c the rain forest

5 I traveled to Disney World with my son last year. I took a lot of pictures of <u>him</u>.
  a Disney World   b picture   c son

6 My brother and I want to see our grandparents in Greece, so our parents bought <u>us</u> tickets to travel there.
  a my brother and I   b grandparents   c parents

9 **INTEGRATE** Complete the paragraphs with the correct object pronouns.

Charles Jencks is an artist and designer. You can learn more about ¹_____ and his work online. In his Garden of Cosmic Speculation, there are many interesting sculptures. Some sculptures are made from plants. You can see pictures of ²_____ on his website.

The Garden of Cosmic Speculation is a fun place, but you can only visit ³_____ one day a year, in April. Tickets cost £10, and you can buy ⁴_____ on the Internet. About 40 percent of the proceeds goes to Maggie's Cancer Caring Centres. Maggie Keswick Jencks, Charles Jencks's wife, died of cancer in 1995, and this charity is named after ⁵_____. The centers help people with cancer, and famous architects helped to design ⁶_____.

10 **WHAT'S YOUR ANGLE?** Which of the four places from the podcast are interesting to you? Why do you like them?

Underground Adventures

1 ACTIVATE Look at the pictures. Describe the caves using four of the words in the box. Compare your words with a partner. Are they the same?

deep	warm	cool	safe	dangerous
bright	dark	scary	pretty	interesting

🍌 Oxford 3000™

> ◎▷**VOCABULARY DEVELOPMENT Adjectives**
>
> An adjective describes a noun. Most adjectives only have one form; they are the same for singular or plural nouns.
>
> a **dark** cave   **dark** caves
>
> Adjectives usually go before a noun or after the verb *be*.
>
> *We found a **deep cave**.*   *Some caves **are dangerous**.*

2 BUILD Put the words in the correct order to complete the sentences.

1 Cave diving _____ (*adventure / exciting / an / is*).
2 It _____ (*safe / is / not*) for beginners, and it _____ (*dangerous / is / often*).
3 Some _____ (*deep / very / caves / are*).
4 It _____ (*dark / underwater / is / inside / an*) cave, so divers take
    _____ (*lights / bright*) with them.
5 There _____ (*some / pretty / are / things*) in the caves.
6 Many divers _____ (*photos / take / interesting*).

3 ◀)) IMPROVE Listen and check your answers to Exercise 2.

4 WHAT'S YOUR ANGLE? Would you like to try cave diving? Why or why not?

> ◎▷**READING SKILL Recognizing and understanding subject-verb-object sentences**
>
> Most English sentences have a **subject** (a noun or a pronoun) and a **verb**. Some subjects can be more than one word.
>
> ***I love** caves.*
> ***My friend and I visited** the caves.*
>
> In some sentences, there is an **object** after the verb. An object can be a noun or a pronoun.
>
> *I study **them**.*
>
> Some **objects** can be more than one word.
>
> *I saw **some interesting and popular caves**.*
>
> If a sentence is hard to understand, identify the **verb** and then the **subject** and **object**.

5 IDENTIFY Read these sentences from the blog post. Identify the parts of the sentence.

1 So every year, I visit a lot of caves.
subject: ___I___ verb: ___visit___ object: ___a lot of caves___

2 In May, I took a day trip to Altamira.
subject: _____ verb: ___took___ object: _____

3 In December, my friend and I took a short trip to Mexico.
subject: _____ verb: _____ object: _____

4 We visited Juxtlahuaca Cave in Guerrero.
subject: _____ verb: _____ object: _____

5 This cave has very old paintings of people and animals.
subject: _____ verb: _____ object: _____

6 I have special lights and a good camera.
subject: _____ verb: _____ object: _____

6 ASSESS Read the blog post. Where did Dan go on his trips? How were the two trips similar? How were they different?

Dan the Caveman

I love caves. I study them. So every year, I visit a lot of caves. Most are small and not very famous, but last year, I saw some interesting and popular caves.

In May, I was in Spain for a friend's wedding, and I took a day trip to the famous caves of Altamira. These caves are in the Cantabrian Mountains near Santander in northern Spain. They are 280 meters deep. On the walls and ceilings, there are paintings of animals and shapes from 13,000 to 11,500 BCE. It was amazing to see them. Some of the paintings are 2 meters across—that's bigger than I am!

These caves are great, but they're hard to visit because Spain wants to protect the paintings. You can see some beautiful images online instead.

In December, my friend and I took a short trip to Mexico, and we visited Juxtlahuaca Cave in Guerrero. We stayed there for four days, and we loved it! Juxtlahuaca Cave is deeper than the Altamira caves. It reaches 2 kilometers into the hills of Guerrero! This cave has very old paintings of people and animals from around 1000 BCE. They are older than any other cave paintings in the Americas. One of the paintings is a 2-meter-tall picture of a man, possibly a king, wearing jaguar skins. It's hard to take pictures in caves because it's dark, but I have special lights and a good camera. What do you think of my photo?

Altamira Caves, Cantabria, Spain

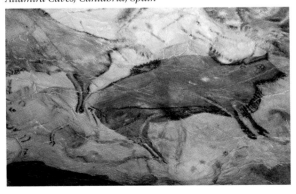

Juxtlahuaca Cave, Guerrero, Mexico

—Adapted from *The Concise Oxford Dictionary of Archaeology*, 2nd ed., by Timothy Darvill

7 WHAT'S YOUR ANGLE? Why do you think people enjoy visiting caves?

> ## GRAMMAR IN CONTEXT Comparative adjectives: Short forms
>
> We use comparative adjectives to describe how one thing or person is different from another thing or person. For short adjectives, we usually form the comparative with *-er*. Add *-er* or *-r* when the adjective ends in *-e*:
>
> long → long**er**
> nice → nic**er**
>
> When the adjective ends in one vowel + one consonant, double the consonant and add *-er*:
>
> big → big**ger**
> hot → hot**ter**
>
> Change *-y* to *–ier*.
>
> scary → scar**ier**
> easy → eas**ier**
>
> We use *than* when we compare two things.
> *That's bigger than I am!*

See Grammar focus on page 168.

8 IDENTIFY Read the blog post again. Choose the correct answer.

		Altamira	Juxtlahuaca
1	Which of Dan's trips was longer?	☐	☐
2	Which of Dan's trips was earlier in the year?	☐	☐
3	Which cave is deeper?	☐	☐
4	Which cave has older paintings?	☐	☐
5	Which place is easier to visit?	☐	☐

9 INTEGRATE Work with a partner. Choose two of the images below. Write three short adjectives to describe each one.

Place 1: _____   **Place 2:** _____

_____   _____

_____   _____

10 INTERACT Work with your partner. Using your adjectives from Exercise 9, write three sentences to compare the two images you chose. Share your sentences with the class.

I think that the old house is scarier than the hotel in the sea.

10.3 I Need a Vacation!

1 ACTIVATE Think of some different types of vacations. What makes each one interesting?

camping: beautiful countryside, I can go hiking

2 ASSESS Read the social media post. Where did each person go for vacation? Which vacation was each person's favorite?

Person	Place 1	Place 2	Favorite
Mary			
Amir			
Sofía			

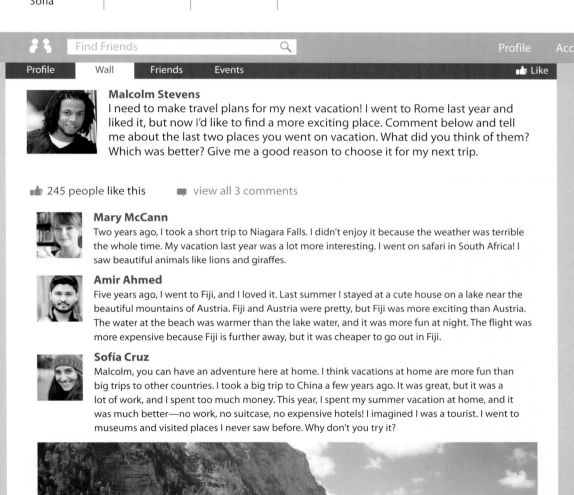

Find Friends

Profile   Account

Profile   Wall   Friends   Events   👍 Like

Malcolm Stevens
I need to make travel plans for my next vacation! I went to Rome last year and liked it, but now I'd like to find a more exciting place. Comment below and tell me about the last two places you went on vacation. What did you think of them? Which was better? Give me a good reason to choose it for my next trip.

👍 245 people like this   💬 view all 3 comments

Mary McCann
Two years ago, I took a short trip to Niagara Falls. I didn't enjoy it because the weather was terrible the whole time. My vacation last year was a lot more interesting. I went on safari in South Africa! I saw beautiful animals like lions and giraffes.

Amir Ahmed
Five years ago, I went to Fiji, and I loved it. Last summer I stayed at a cute house on a lake near the beautiful mountains of Austria. Fiji and Austria were pretty, but Fiji was more exciting than Austria. The water at the beach was warmer than the lake water, and it was more fun at night. The flight was more expensive because Fiji is further away, but it was cheaper to go out in Fiji.

Sofía Cruz
Malcolm, you can have an adventure here at home. I think vacations at home are more fun than big trips to other countries. I took a big trip to China a few years ago. It was great, but it was a lot of work, and I spent too much money. This year, I spent my summer vacation at home, and it was much better—no work, no suitcase, no expensive hotels! I imagined I was a tourist. I went to museums and visited places I never saw before. Why don't you try it?

3 WHAT'S YOUR ANGLE? Do you like to stay at home for your vacation? Why or why not? What adventure can you have in the area where you live?

 GRAMMAR IN CONTEXT Comparative adjectives: Long and irregular forms

We use comparative adjectives to describe how one thing or person is different from another thing or person. For long adjectives (three or more syllables and some with two syllables), we form the comparative with *more* + adjective.

interesting → more interesting   boring → more boring

We use comparative adjectives with *than*.

*Fiji was **more exciting than** Austria.*

The adjectives *good*, *bad*, and *far* are irregular. The comparative form is a different word.

good → better   bad → worse   far → farther or further

Some short adjectives take the word *more* and not the ending *-er*.

fun → more fun   bored → more bored

See Grammar focus on page 168.

4 DEVELOP Complete the sentences about the social media post.

1   The water at the __beach_____ in Fiji was _warmer than__ the water in the lake in Austria.
2   Malcolm wants to take a trip to a _____ exciting place than _____.
3   Mary's safari in South _____ was _____ interesting _____ her trip to Niagara Falls.
4   Amir's flight to Fiji was more _____ than his flight to Austria because Fiji was _____ away.
5   Amir thought that _____ was _____ fun at night than _____.
6   Sofía thinks that her vacation at home was a lot _____ than her big trip to China.

 WRITING SKILL Using adjectives to make your writing more interesting

When you write a description, you want to "paint a picture" for your readers. Use adjectives to help them see what you saw and feel what you felt. Compare these two descriptions. Which is more interesting?

Description 1: I stayed at a house on a lake near the mountains.
Description 2: I stayed at a cute house on a lake near the beautiful mountains of Austria.

5 IDENTIFY How many adjectives can you find in the social media post? Compare your list with a partner's.

6 USE Look at the pictures and write the sentences again. Add adjectives to make them more interesting.

1   My friends visited a village near a forest.   _My friends visited a pretty village near a large forest._
2   They stayed in a house.   _____
3   There was a beach next to our hotel.   _____
4   We loved the weather.   _____
5   The building is on a street.   _____

7 VOCABULARY Complete the text with the correct words.

winter	trip	vacation	summer	break	suitcase

 Oxford 3000™

It's important to work hard, but it's also important to go on ¹_____. We need time to have fun and do things we like. Sometimes it's fun to stay home and spend time with our friends and family, but other times it's great to pack a ²_____ and take a ³_____ somewhere interesting by train or by plane.

Maybe you don't have two weeks or a month to travel. That's OK—you can go on a short ⁴_____. Spend a weekend visiting a friend or family member. You don't have to go far!

Many families go on a ⁵_____ vacation together because their children aren't in school in July and August. They go camping or go to the beach. Some people like snow sports and cold weather. They take a ⁶_____ vacation and go skiing.

8 WHAT'S YOUR ANGLE? Answer the questions in complete sentences. Compare your answers with a partner.

1 How often do you go on vacation? *I go on vacation every year.*
2 Is it better to go on one long vacation or to go on a lot of short breaks?
3 Is it more interesting to take trips to places near your home or far away? Why?
4 Where do you like to spend summer vacations? What about winter vacations?
5 How many suitcases do you usually take on a trip?

9 PREPARE Think of two trips you took. Make notes on the places, the activities, and your opinions. Include adjectives.

Budapest, Hungary: exciting, old buildings, busy streets, excellent food
Place 1:
Place 2:

10 WRITE Use your notes to write a reply to Malcolm. Compare the two places you visited and recommend one to Malcolm.

11 IMPROVE Read your post and correct any spelling or grammar mistakes.

Does your post…
■ answer Malcolm's question?
■ use adjectives to make your description interesting?
■ include comparative adjectives?
■ use the correct forms for comparative adjectives?

12 SHARE Exchange posts with a partner. What do you think of the places your partner described?

The Tiber river in Rome, Italy

1 ACTIVATE Think about the last time you suggested an activity to a friend. When was it, and what did you say? Did your friend agree with your idea? How did your friend respond?

2 ▶ **ASSESS** Watch the video. Choose the correct answers. Questions may have more than one answer.

1 Where does Andy want to go?
  a Phoenix, Arizona
  b Sedona, Arizona
  c the Grand Canyon
  d Las Vegas, Nevada

2 Where does Max want to go?
  a Phoenix, Arizona
  b Sedona, Arizona
  c the Grand Canyon
  d Las Vegas, Nevada

3 Where do they finally decide to go together?
  a Phoenix, Arizona
  b Sedona, Arizona
  c the Grand Canyon
  d Las Vegas, Nevada

3 ▶ **IDENTIFY** Watch the video again. Who said what: Max or Andy?

1 I found us the best place to go for our vacation in April. _____
2 What about somewhere quieter and more relaxing? _____
3 I can think of nicer places to go. _____
4 What about this: We fly to Phoenix, Arizona. _____
5 Fine, but can we stop at the Grand Canyon after that? _____
6 OK...it's a deal! _____
7 Now that sounds like a much better plan. _____

ENGLISH FOR REAL

120

When you want to suggest an activity, use expressions like:

Why don't we...?
I have an idea. Let's...
What about...?
How about...?

You can respond to a suggestion in different ways.

Positive opinion	Negative opinion
Good idea!	*Really? No, thanks.*
OK! That sounds great.	*Hmm, I'm not (so) sure.*
It's a deal!	*I don't know (about that).*

You can also respond with a different opinion or suggestion.

I can think of nicer places to go.

That sounds good, but I think _____ is more interesting.
Hmm. What about...?
How about...?

4 **ANALYZE** Look at the statements again from Exercise 3. Which three make a suggestion? Which give opinions?

5 **WHAT'S YOUR ANGLE?** Choose a place you'd like to travel. Write three reasons why this is a good place to go.

Place: _____

Reason 1: _____

Reason 2: _____

Reason 3: _____

6 **INTEGRATE** Which phrases can you use to suggest this place to a friend for your next vacation? Make notes.

Let's go to Hawaii for vacation.

7 **INTERACT** Work with a partner. Imagine you are traveling together. Make your suggestion, and then give your opinion of your partner's place. Together, make a decision about where to go.

Student A: I have an idea. Let's go to Cancún for vacation.

Student B: Hmm. I don't know. I think Montréal, Canada, is a better place to go.

Student A: I'm not sure about that. Cancún is warmer and has nice beaches…

GO ONLINE
to create your own version
of the English For Real video.

1 ACTIVATE Read the ads. Before you listen to a conversation between a travel agent and a customer, think about the words and phrases you might hear.

How much does it cost? Where is the hotel?

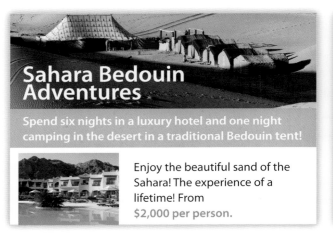

Sahara Bedouin Adventures

Spend six nights in a luxury hotel and one night camping in the desert in a traditional Bedouin tent!

Enjoy the beautiful sand of the Sahara! The experience of a lifetime! From $2,000 per person.

Winter Mountain Adventures

Do you love skiing?

Would you like to try camping in cold weather?

Join us for a Winter Mountain Adventure!

Five days and **four nights** to remember!

2 **IDENTIFY** Listen. Which trip does the woman choose? Why?

PRONUNCIATION SKILL Comparatives with weak form of *than*

We usually put stress on the most important words in a sentence. In a comparative sentence, we often stress the things we are comparing. Sometimes we stress the comparative adjective. The word *than* is less important, so we don't stress it. We say it quickly.

Swimming is more fun thən skiing.

3 **NOTICE** Listen and identify the words that are stressed the most. Then listen again and repeat.

1 (Long) trips are (better) than (short) trips.
2 Today is hotter than yesterday.
3 Mountains are more beautiful than deserts.
4 Swimming is more fun than skiing.
5 The bus is cheaper than the plane.

SPEAKING Making comparisons

Use comparisons to give more information about a topic or help your listener understand your opinion.
*The desert is **drier than** the mountains.*
*I think the desert is **more beautiful than** the mountains.*

To say how you feel about two places or things, you can use *I like X better than Y.*
*I like warm weather **better than** cold weather.*

You don't always need to use *than*:
*Which is **more fun**, the beach or a lake?*　　*I think the beach is **more fun**.*

4 WHAT'S YOUR ANGLE? Would you like to visit the desert or the mountains? Think of some questions about the vacations.

5 INTERACT With a partner, role-play a conversation between a travel agent and a customer. Explain which trip you like better and why. Switch roles.

11 Learning

How are the students learning?

Do you like learning new things?

Is learning or teaching more difficult?

BEHIND THE PHOTO

REAL-WORLD GOAL

Watch a video online to learn how to do something

1 Choose the answers that are true for you. Add your own answer.

1 I like learning *a new language* / *a new sport* / *a new dance* / _____.

2 I like studying *at home* / *at the library* / *in a coffee shop* / _____.

3 When I want to learn about something, I *read a book about it* / *go on the Internet* / *ask someone about it* / _____.

4 When I meet new people, I learn about them by *asking them questions* / *spending time with them* / *looking them up on social media* / _____.

5 I learn skills by *taking a class* / *watching an online video* / *asking for help* / _____.

2 Share your answers with a partner.

11.1 Not All Fun and Games

1 ACTIVATE What's your dream job? What skills do you need to learn for this job, or what do you need to study?

My dream job is to be a pilot. I need to learn about flying.

> **VOCABULARY DEVELOPMENT Study collocations**
>
> Use these common verbs with nouns to describe study activities.
>
> | | |
> |---|---|
> | *take...* | *a class / a test / notes / a break* |
> | *do...* | *well / homework* |
> | *make...* | *a mistake* |
> | *write...* | *a paper* |
> | *learn...* | *about (something)* |
> | *try...* | *to (do something)* |

2 IDENTIFY Decide if each underlined word is correct or incorrect. Write the correct word.

1 I love learning <u>of</u> geography.   correct   incorrect
2 Some students don't <u>do</u> notes in class.   correct   incorrect
3 Would you like to <u>make</u> a ten-minute break?   correct   incorrect
4 I <u>tried</u> to study last night, but I was very tired.   correct   incorrect
5 She speaks English well. She doesn't <u>do</u> a lot of mistakes.   correct   incorrect
6 I <u>take</u> classes at the local college.   correct   incorrect

3 INTEGRATE Write five sentences about your studies. Use the study collocations and adverbs of frequency.

every day / week / month	always	often	sometimes	never

I never write papers. I always try to understand the teacher.

4 ASSESS Look at the image. What kind of school do you think she goes to? Do you think she's having fun? Read the email and check.

✉

From: Sam

Subject: Game designing isn't all fun and games!

Hello, Val!

How are you doing?

I'm taking a break from my homework to tell you about my first month at college. Wow! The Game Design program is harder than high school! It's not all fun and games—it's serious work! And I'm not doing that well. 😔

I'm trying! I'm going to all my classes, I'm doing all my homework, and I'm studying hard, but I just took my first test in Programming 101, and I made a lot of mistakes. Also, this week in Digital Painting class we're learning about painting people. I can paint buildings and animals all right, but I can't paint people very well! It's really hard... BUT I know I can be a good game designer! I have a lot of good ideas, and I'm good at learning new skills. I just need to work hard and try to do better.

I need to get back to work soon. I'm writing a paper about famous video games for my History of Gaming class. Also, I have a big test on Tuesday in my Introduction to Game Design class. Wish me luck!

Love, Sam

5 WHAT'S YOUR ANGLE? Would you like to study at the game designing school? Why or why not? What kind of college or school would you like to go to?

No, I wouldn't like to study at the game designing school because I don't like computer games. I'd like to go to cooking school.

GRAMMAR IN CONTEXT Present continuous: Positive and negative

We use the present continuous to talk about actions happening now or to talk about the situation now. We form the present continuous with: Subject + *am / are / is* + *-ing* form.

Happening now: I'm taking a break from my homework.
Situation now: This week we're learning about painting people.

We form the negative present continuous with: Subject + *am / are / is* + *not* + *-ing* form.

I'm not doing that well.
We aren't playing a lot of games.

See Grammar focus on page 169.

6 IDENTIFY Read the email again. Complete the information. Use full sentences where possible.

1 Who is Sam writing to?
  She's writing to her friend Val.

2 Sam is trying to do well at school. Write three things she is doing at school that show she is trying:

    a _____

    b _____

    c _____

3 What four classes is Sam taking?

    a _____

    b _____

    c _____

    d _____

4 What is she writing a paper about?

    _____

7 WHAT'S YOUR ANGLE? Think about what you're studying. What is one thing you're doing and one thing you're learning?

I'm studying English and fashion design. I'm trying to improve my speaking skills. Now we're learning about the present continuous.

Students at the Kiton Tailoring School in Arzano, Italy

8 PREPARE Imagine you are studying game design, or choose one of the schools in the advertisements. Think about these questions and take notes.

   1   What do people study at this school?

   2   What activities do they do?

   3   What are the classes like? (use adjectives: *fun, difficult,* etc.)

HOME RUN

SPORTS ACADEMY

Learn about the sports business, or train to be a coach, a personal trainer, a teacher, a sports writer, or a sports radio / TV host!

Davis
Doughnut College

Learn to make perfect doughnuts!

 WRITING SKILL Writing informally with contractions

When you write a paper for class, or a business letter, use the long form of the verbs *be* and *do*. When you write an email or message to a friend or someone you know well, you can use contractions (short forms).

I ~~am learning~~ how to make doughnuts.	I'm learning how to make doughnuts.
The classes ~~are not~~ hard.	The classes aren't hard.
We ~~do not~~ have a lot of homework.	We don't have a lot of homework.

---

9 🔊 **DEVELOP** Listen to the sentences with the long form of *be* or *do*. Rewrite the sentences using contractions.

   1   <u>I'm not having fun at college.</u>

   2   _____

   3   _____

   4   _____

   5   _____

   6   _____

   7   _____

10 WRITE Write an email to a friend or family member. Tell them what you are studying and how you are doing. Use the ideas from Exercise 8 or your real studies.

11 IMPROVE Read your email. Check your spelling and grammar.

Did you…

   ■ use the present continuous to talk about what you're doing now?

   ■ use the correct form and spelling of the present continuous verbs?

   ■ use contractions?

12 SHARE Swap emails with a partner. Give your partner feedback.

1   ACTIVATE Look at the images. What are the people learning about? How are they learning?

2   IDENTIFY Brainstorm some other ways that people learn about something or how to do something.

watching a video online

 READING SKILL Skimming

Skimming is looking at a text quickly to get the main ideas. When you skim, you don't read all of the words. You can do this when you want to understand quickly what a text is about.

3   ASSESS Skim the article for the main ideas. Then complete the statements.

1   The article is about *learning styles / good learners / bad learners.*
2   There are *three / four / five* kinds of learners.
3   Visual learners learn best by *seeing / doing / listening.*
4   Auditory learners learn best by *seeing / doing / listening.*
5   Kinesthetic learners learn best by *seeing / doing / listening.*

4 **INTERACT** What kind of learner are you? Do a class survey. How many people are visual, auditory, and kinesthetic leaners?

What's Your Learning Style?

Learning is fun, and it's important, too! But we all learn in different ways. Here are the three common types of learners.

Visual learners

For visual learners, seeing is the best way to learn. These learners do well in lessons with text, pictures, or video. They don't do well in lessons where the teacher is only speaking with no visual aids. Showing them the information helps them remember it better.

Auditory learners

For auditory learners, listening is the best way to understand something. They like to hear their teacher explain things and give examples. Reading out loud to "hear" the information is helpful. Talking to native speakers is a good activity for auditory language learners.

Kinesthetic learners

For kinesthetic learners, *doing* something is the most important way to learn it. These learners like to move around or to use their hands to work on something. They do well in lessons where a teacher shows them *how* to do something and then they have the chance to try it.

—Adapted from *A Dictionary of Education*, 2nd ed., edited by Susan Wallace

 GRAMMAR IN CONTEXT Using *-ing* forms as subjects

We can use the *-ing* form of a verb as a noun. It can be the subject of a sentence.
Seeing is the best way to learn.

See Grammar focus on page 169.

5 **IDENTIFY** Find the seven *-ing* forms of verbs used as subjects in the article.

6 **USE** Look at the pictures. Write 2–3 *-ing* verbs to describe the actions in each picture.

7 🔊 **DEVELOP** Listen and complete the sentences about the pictures from Exercise 6. Use -ing forms.

1 Picture 1: _____ is fun! _____ is one way to learn how to do it.
2 Picture 2: _____ is always interesting. _____ is the best way to learn about other countries.
3 Picture 3: _____ can teach us a lot about the world. _____ helps scientists with their work.

8 **VOCABULARY** Take the questionnaire.

What's Your Learning Style?

	always	sometimes	never
V I understand information better when I can watch a video about it.	☐	☐	☐
_____ I learn well when the teacher speaks and explains things to us.	☐	☐	☐
_____ I learn best when the teacher shows us how to do something and then asks us to do it.	☐	☐	☐
_____ I like when the teacher gives examples on the board.	☐	☐	☐
_____ I can learn a new song by listening to it a few times.	☐	☐	☐
_____ Sitting through an hour-long class is boring. I need to get up and move around!	☐	☐	☐
_____ When I learn a new word, I need to see how it's spelled.	☐	☐	☐
_____ Working through problems is easier when I talk about them with another student.	☐	☐	☐
_____ Playing a game is a great way for me to learn and remember a lesson.	☐	☐	☐

🔑 Oxford 3000™

9 **IDENTIFY** Read the questions in the questionnaire. Which questions relate to visual, auditory, or kinesthetic learners? Look back at the article on page 128 for help. Write *V*, *A*, or *K* next to each item.

10 **WHAT'S YOUR ANGLE?** Write three good activities for learning English based on your learning style. Share with a partner. Can you give them some more ideas?

I'm an auditory learner. Listening to music in English is a good activity for learning English.

11.3 Making a Change

1 ACTIVATE In your opinion, what makes people happy in their jobs? Why are some people unhappy? Talk to a partner.

2 ▶ **ASSESS** Watch the video. Answer the questions.

1 What are Sarita's two jobs?
2 Does she like her jobs? How do you know?

3 VOCABULARY Look at the vocabulary for talking about work. Find three things Sarita does and three things she doesn't do.

learn new skills	work in an office	look for a new job
go to meetings	have a part-time job	make (people) happy
work for a large company	help people	make (a lot of) money

🔑 Oxford 3000™

4 WHAT'S YOUR ANGLE? Look at the statements. Choose the ones that are true for you. Share with the class.

☐ 1 I work in an office.
☐ 2 I work for a large company.
☐ 3 I need to learn new skills.
☐ 4 I want to look for a new job.
☐ 5 I have a part-time job.
☐ 6 My job makes me happy.
☐ 7 I go to lots of meetings.
☐ 8 Making a lot of money is more important than loving your job.
☐ 9 I'd like to get a job that helps people.
☐ 10 I learn something at work every day.

5 ASSESS Look at the picture.

1 Where does the woman work?
2 Do you think she loves what she does? Why or why not?

LISTENING SKILL Understanding the structure of a talk or radio program

Talks and radio programs usually have the same structure. The introduction presents the topic. Then the speaker gives information and examples to answer questions about the topic. The conclusion gives a summary and makes a final statement about the topic. Understanding the structure helps you to focus and plan your listening.

6 IDENTIFY Read the information from a radio program. Then match each statement to a part of the structure.

1	Introduction	a	Mindy talks about why she isn't looking for a new job now.
2	Example 1	b	The narrator talks about things we can learn from Mindy.
3	Example 2	c	The narrator tells us that many people have jobs they don't like.
4	Example 3	d	Mindy talks about how she's trying to be happier at work.
5	Conclusion	e	Mindy tells us why she doesn't like her job.

7 🔊 **INTEGRATE** Listen to the radio program and check your answers to Exercise 6.

8 WHAT'S YOUR ANGLE? Do you know someone in Mindy's situation? Do you think her plan is good?

GRAMMAR IN CONTEXT Present continuous: Questions

We form *yes/no* questions in the present continuous with: *Am / Are / Is* + subject + -*ing* form?
Is *your job **making** you happy?*

We can answer with a short form.
*Yes, it **is**.*
*No, it **isn't**.*

We form *wh-* questions in the present continuous with: Question word + *am / are / is* + subject + -*ing* form?
What is *she **doing** about it?*

See Grammar focus on page 169.

9 INTEGRATE Complete the questions about the radio program in the present continuous.

1 Why _isn't_____ Mindy _looking_____ for a new job?
2 (make) _____ Mindy's job _____ her happy?
3 (try) _____ she _____ to change her situation?
4 (do) What _____ she _____ during lunch breaks?
5 (learn) What kinds of skills _____ Mindy _____ on the job?
6 (take) What class _____ she _____ at night?

10 INTERACT Work with a partner. Ask and answer the questions from Exercise 9. Use short answers where possible.

Why isn't Mindy looking for a new job?
Because she wants more experience.

11 WHAT'S YOUR ANGLE? Think of something in your life you are trying to change. What are you doing about it?

I want to buy a house. I'm working part time to make money.

11.4 How about You?

1 ACTIVATE Read the statements and think about your conversation style. Choose the answers that are true for you.

1 In a conversation…
   a I talk more than the other person.
   b the other person talks more than I do.
   c we both talk the same amount of time.
   d the amount I speak depends on who I'm talking to.

2 Most of the time…
   a I talk about myself.
   b I ask questions.
   c I talk about myself and ask questions.
   d the amount I speak depends on what we're talking about.

3 When someone is telling a story…
   a I listen quietly.
   b I listen and ask questions.
   c I stop them and give my opinion.
   d my response depends on who is talking.

2 ▶ ASSESS Watch the video. Who starts the conversation? Who joins the conversation? What do they talk about?

REAL-WORLD ENGLISH Turn taking

When we have a conversation, we take turns. We use some words and phrases to begin our turn or to give the other person a turn to talk.

Starting a conversation

What are you up to?
What's happening?

Giving the other person a turn

How about you? / What about you? / And you?
So, (what do you think about…? / why are you taking that class…?)

It's good to show that we're listening to the other person when we are hearing something. We use words and sounds to do this.

Listening and reacting

Mm-hmm. / Yeah. / Uh-huh. / Hmm / Wow. / Oh. / Really? / Cool.

3 ▶ **IDENTIFY** Watch the video again. Listen for these phrases. Who said what?

1 What are you up to?   _____

2 How about you?   _____

3 How's it going?   _____

4 So...why are you taking Latin?   _____

5 Oh, really?   _____

6 Oh...cool!   _____

7 Mm-hmm.   _____

4 **ANALYZE** Think about the phrases from Exercise 3. Decide if they start a conversation (*S*), give the other person a turn (*G*), or show you are listening (*L*). Compare your answers with a partner.

5 **INTERACT** Work with a partner. Choose a topic to talk about and make some notes.

- ■ your English studies
- ■ your job
- ■ your favorite sport or activity
- ■ your own idea

6 **INTEGRATE** Start a conversation with a partner about your chosen topic. Take turns talking and listening. Use phrases from the box for starting a conversation, giving the other person a turn, and listening and reacting.

Student A: Hey. What are you up to?

Student B: Not much. I'm reading this interesting book. It's about…

Student A: So, are you watching any good TV shows?

Student B: Yes, I'm watching *Mozart in the Jungle*. How about you?

GO ONLINE
to create your own version
of the English For Real video.

133

1   **ACTIVATE** Look at the picture and read the information in the Speaking box. Imagine some questions the men can ask each other.

> ### SPEAKING Asking and answering personal questions
>
> When you know someone well and want to ask questions about his or her life, family, and so on, you can use these phrases:
>
> *How are you doing?*
> *I'm doing great, thanks! How about you?*
> *I'm doing well, too. How's your family?*
>
> You can use different tenses to answer the questions.
>
> *What are you doing now? I left my old job, and now I'm working in a school. I'm a math teacher.*

2   **IDENTIFY** Listen to Tony and Al's conversation. Choose the correct answers.

1   Tony is *still working* / *isn't working*.
2   Al and his wife *work* / *don't work*.
3   Al and his wife are taking *a language class* / *a cooking class*.
4   They'd like to *travel to* / *move to* Portugal.
5   Tony is *taking a class* / *thinking about taking* a class.

> ### PRONUNCIATION SKILL Contractions with *be*
>
> When we speak, we usually use contractions. Contractions are pronounced differently from the long forms.
>
> **She is** not working.   **She's** not working. / She **isn't** working.

3   **NOTICE** Decide which sentences you hear. Then listen and repeat.

1   a   She is not working.   b   She's not working.
2   a   We are studying English.   b   We're studying English.
3   a   He is not living in London.   b   He isn't living in London.
4   a   They are at school now.   b   They're at school now.
5   a   You are looking good.   b   You're looking good.

4   **WHAT'S YOUR ANGLE?** Think about meeting an old friend. What questions would you ask him or her? Make notes.

5   **INTEGRATE** Work with a partner. Imagine you are old friends and you see each other at a coffee shop. Ask and answer your questions.

Student A: Hey, (name), is that you?
Student B: Hey! Good to see you! How are you doing?

12 Activities

Describe the scene.

What fun activities can
you do outside?

What can you do when
it's raining?

BEHIND THE PHOTO

**REAL-
WORLD
GOAL**

Invite a new friend to
do something with you

**1 Think about your favorite activities. Complete the statements so they are
true for you.**

1   When I feel bored, I usually _____.

2   In my free time, I love _____.

3   My favorite thing to do on vacation is _____.

4   On weekends, I often _____.

5   After class today, I'd like to _____.

2 Share your ideas with a partner.

What's Your Circus Maximus?

1 ACTIVATE Match the activities to the pictures. Do you like doing these things in your free time?

1 ____meeting up with friends
2 ____meeting new people
3 ____making things
4 ____riding a horse

5 ____shopping
6 ____watching sports
7 ____playing a game
8 ____using social media

a

b

c

d

e

f

g

h

2 IDENTIFY Brainstorm some more popular hobbies.

3 WHAT'S YOUR ANGLE? What's your favorite hobby? When do you do it?

My favorite hobby is painting. I do it in my free time.

4 **ASSESS** Read the encyclopedia entry. What was the Circus Maximus?

> **READING SKILL** Guessing meaning from context

The context of a word is the sentence or paragraph that it's in. When you don't know a word, its context can sometimes help you understand its meaning.

*In **ancient** Rome, a **circus** was a place where people came to watch **chariot races**.*

You can guess the meaning of *ancient*, *circus*, and *chariot races* from the context. For example, there is a photo of a chariot race in the article. The word *circus* is defined as "a place where people came to watch chariot races." You can guess that *ancient* means "very old, a long time ago" because of the past tense verbs, the photos, and your knowledge (we don't have chariot races today).

Circus Maximus

In ancient Rome, one of the greatest empires in history, a circus was a place where people came to watch chariot races. The first, largest, and most famous of all the ancient Roman circuses was the Circus Maximus. It was first built in the sixth century BCE by the king Tarquinius Priscus. Later, other Roman rulers, including Julius Caesar, made it bigger and more modern. It measured 621 meters long and 118 meters across and could fit 250,000 spectators.

As well as chariot races, people also came to watch other games and shows at the circus, such as gladiator fights. People loved watching the sports and shows, but they came to the circus for other reasons, too. Because the circus was the biggest and most popular place to go in Rome, it was the best place to meet up with friends or meet new people. And all around the circus, people sold food and merchandise, so the circus was also a great place for people to shop and to eat.

The circus area is now a public park. The band Genesis played a concert there for 500,000 people in 2007.

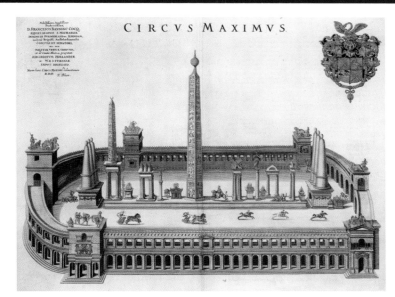

chariots racing

gladiators fight

—Adapted from *A Dictionary of Sports Studies* (1ed.) by Alan Tomlinson

5 USE Read the text again. Match the words to their meaning based on the context.

1	century	a	new
2	spectator	b	100 years
3	modern	c	things that you can buy, such as T-shirts at a concert
4	ruler	d	a person who watches sports at a stadium
5	gladiator	e	king or leader of a country or empire, like the Roman Empire
6	merchandise	f	a person who fought in a stadium in ancient Rome

6 IDENTIFY Name four activities people did at the Circus Maximus. What is the area used for now?

GRAMMAR IN CONTEXT Superlative adjectives

We use superlative adjectives to describe how a person or thing compares to the group it belongs to. We use *the* before a superlative.

The first, largest, and most famous of all the ancient Roman circuses was the Circus Maximus.

For short adjectives, add *-est* or *-st*. For long adjectives, we use *most* + adjective.

long → longest
big → biggest
interesting → most interesting
nice → nicest
funny → funniest
exciting → most exciting

The adjectives *good*, *bad* and *far* are irregular. The superlative form is a different word.

good → best
bad → worst
far → farthest or furthest

See Grammar focus on page 170.

7 IDENTIFY Find all the examples of superlative adjectives in the reading.

8 **DEVELOP** Listen and complete the sentences with the superlatives you hear.

1   Main Street in the city center is __the best__ place to go shopping.
2   In my area, the football stadium is _____ place for famous bands to play concerts.
3   _____ sport where I live is hockey.
4   For me, the _____ exercise activity is mountain climbing.
5   _____ restaurant in my town is Chez Louis.
6   _____ place for me to go is the shopping mall.
7   For me, _____ hobby is watching TV.

9 WHAT'S YOUR ANGLE? Change the statements from Activity 8 to be true for you and where you live. Share your ideas with a partner.

Derby Street is the best place to go shopping.

10 INTERACT Brainstorm with the class. What are some modern examples of events that bring a lot of people together? Which ones are special to your country?

The Super Bowl is really popular in the United States. Everyone loves American football!

12.2 It's Party Time!

1 🔊 **ACTIVATE** Complete the sentences. Then listen and check your answers.

| cake | party | sandwiches | invite | birthday | ice cream | holidays |

♟ Oxford 3000™

I love ¹_____, especially Thanksgiving, Halloween, and Independence Day. I always have fun with my family and friends.

I usually do something fun for my ²_____, which is May 12th. Sometimes I have a small ³_____ at my house. I ⁴_____ my friends and family. I usually get some pizza or ⁵_____ for people to eat. Then later we eat ⁶_____ or ⁷_____.

2 **WHAT'S YOUR ANGLE?** Discuss with a partner.

1 What holidays do you celebrate at home?
2 Do you have parties? Who do you invite, and what do you eat?
3 What other ways do you celebrate?

3 **ASSESS** Read the invitation. What is the party for?

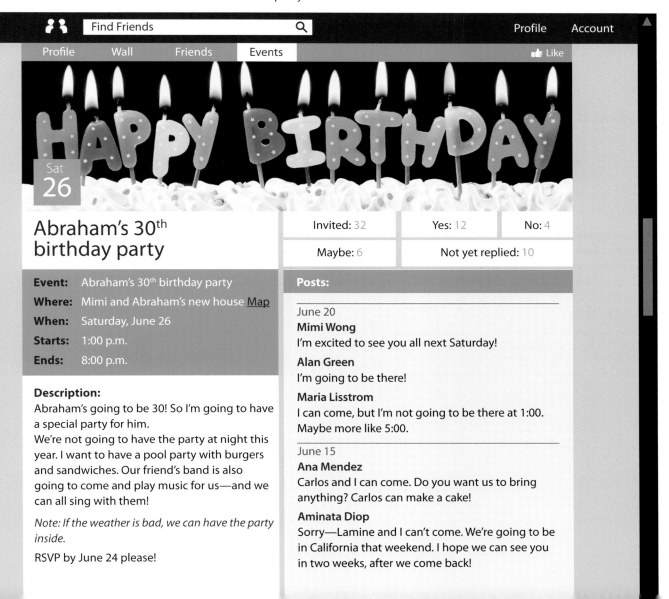

| Find Friends 🔍 | | Profile | Account |

| Profile | Wall | Friends | **Events** | 👍 Like |

HAPPY BIRTHDAY

Sat 26

Abraham's 30th birthday party

| Invited: 32 | Yes: 12 | No: 4 |
| Maybe: 6 | Not yet replied: 10 | |

Event: Abraham's 30th birthday party
Where: Mimi and Abraham's new house Map
When: Saturday, June 26
Starts: 1:00 p.m.
Ends: 8:00 p.m.

Description:
Abraham's going to be 30! So I'm going to have a special party for him.
We're not going to have the party at night this year. I want to have a pool party with burgers and sandwiches. Our friend's band is also going to come and play music for us—and we can all sing with them!

Note: If the weather is bad, we can have the party inside.

RSVP by June 24 please!

Posts:

June 20
Mimi Wong
I'm excited to see you all next Saturday!

Alan Green
I'm going to be there!

Maria Lisstrom
I can come, but I'm not going to be there at 1:00. Maybe more like 5:00.

June 15
Ana Mendez
Carlos and I can come. Do you want us to bring anything? Carlos can make a cake!

Aminata Diop
Sorry—Lamine and I can't come. We're going to be in California that weekend. I hope we can see you in two weeks, after we come back!

139

GRAMMAR IN CONTEXT *Going to*: Future plans

We use *be* + *going to* to talk about future plans.

I'm going to have a special party for Abraham's birthday this year.

We form negative sentences with: Subject + *be* + *not* + *going to* + infinitive.

We're not going to have the party at night this year.

See Grammar focus on page 170.

4 IDENTIFY Read the invitation again. Are the statements *True* or *False*?

1 The party is going to start at 8:00.	True	False
2 There is going to be a band at the party.	True	False
3 Aminata and her husband aren't going to be at the party.	True	False
4 Mimi is going to make a cake.	True	False
5 Alan is going to be at the party.	True	False

5 INTEGRATE Use the prompts and the correct form of *be going to* to write full sentences.

1 he / not have a birthday party   *He's not going to have a birthday party.*

2 I / meet my friends / after class   _____

3 I / not cook dinner / tonight   _____

4 we / see a movie / later   _____

5 she / visit her brother / this weekend   _____

6 we / not go on vacation / this summer   _____

6 WHAT'S YOUR ANGLE? What was the last party you went to? Was it fun? Why or why not?

The last party I went to was my friend's New Year's Eve party. It was fun because all of our friends were there and we danced a lot.

7 PREPARE You're going to have a party at your house. Make notes about...

1 what holiday or birthday the party is for: _____

2 who you're going to invite: _____

3 what food you're going to make or buy: _____

4 when the party is going to be: _____

5 2–3 fun things you're going to do: _____

WRITING SKILL Adding detail using time expressions

Time expressions tell you when events happen, are happening, or are going to happen. They make your writing clearer. They include dates, times, and phrases like *last week, this weekend, tonight, tomorrow, on Friday,* and *next week.* Time expressions usually go at the end of a sentence.

My birthday is next month.
They're going to leave at 2:30.

8 IDENTIFY Find at least five time expressions in the invitation from Exercise 3.

9 INTEGRATE Create an invitation like the one in Exercise 3. Use your notes from Exercise 7. Include time expressions.

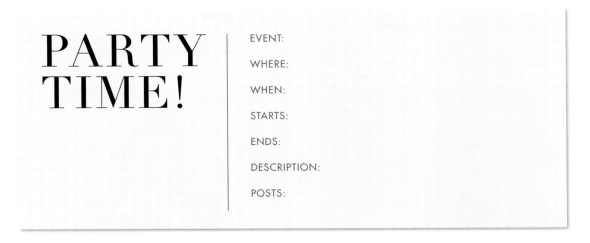

PARTY TIME!

EVENT:

WHERE:

WHEN:

STARTS:

ENDS:

DESCRIPTION:

POSTS:

10 IMPROVE Read your invitation. Check for errors.

Did you...

- use *going to* correctly to describe your party plans?
- include time expressions?
- use correct spelling?

11 SHARE Exchange invitations with a partner. Reply "yes" or "no" to the invitation and add a comment. Share with the class.

A wedding reception in Rome, Italy

141

1 **ACTIVATE** Look at the images. Brainstorm some words to describe the people.

The optimist is happy. He's having fun.

Are You an Optimist or a Pessimist?

Optimist

Pessimist

VOCABULARY DEVELOPMENT Future time expressions

Use *in* and *next* to talk about future time.

in: *in the future*   *in an hour*   *in two years*
next: *next week*   *next month*   *next year*

We can also use *tonight, tomorrow,* and *this.*

this: *this morning*   *this afternoon*   *this evening*

Time expressions can go at the beginning or end of a sentence. When they go at the beginning, we add a comma.

*I'm going to finish school **in two months**.*
***In the future**, I'm going to be a doctor.*

2 **USE** Choose the correct answer.

1 In the *future / year / hour*, I'm going to buy a house.
2 This *today / afternoon / two weeks*, I'm going to meet my friend.
3 She's going to start college next *years / future / year*.
4 I'm going to travel to Europe in *month / a month / next month*.
5 *Next / In / Tonight* Friday, I'm going to see a basketball game.
6 My friend and I are going to go camping this *weeks / tomorrow / weekend*.

3 **WHAT'S YOUR ANGLE?** Think about your plans for the next month. Write five sentences using five of the future time expressions.

Next week, I'm going to have dinner with some friends.

LISTENING SKILL Understanding different voices

Everybody has a different voice. Some voices are harder to understand, so
practice is useful. What affects someone's voice? Think about these questions.
Is the speaker male or female?
Does the speaker sound younger or older?
Is his or her voice high or deep, quiet or loud?
Does the person speak fast or slowly?
How does the speaker feel? (e.g., excited, bored, etc.)

4 🔊 **IDENTIFY** You are going to hear an interviewer talk to two students. Before you
listen to the whole interview, listen to some sentences and match them to the images.
Who says what?

1 ____
2 ____
3 ____
4 ____
5 ____
6 ____

a   b   c

5 🔊 **INTERACT** Listen to the full interview. Discuss with a partner.

1   Which person is an optimist, the young man or the young woman? Why do you think so?

2   Is one of them a pessimist? Why or why not?

GRAMMAR IN CONTEXT *Going to*: **Questions**

We form *yes/no* questions with: *Be* + subject + *going to* + infinitive.

Are you going to finish school soon?

We form *wh-* questions with: Question word + *be* + subject + *going to* + infinitive?

What are you going to do now?

See Grammar focus on page 170.

6 **DEVELOP** Complete the questions about the interview with the correct form of *be going to*.

1   What _____ they _____ talk about?

2   When _____ the young woman _____ finish school?

3   _____ the students _____ go traveling?

4   _____ the young woman _____ be a writer?

5   Where _____ the young man _____ look for a job?

7 🔊 **IDENTIFY** Choose the correct answers to the questions from Exercise 6. Then listen
again and check.

1   a   an interview   b   the future
2   a   next year   b   in two months
3   a   No, they're not.   b   Yes, they are.
4   a   Yes, she is.   b   No, she isn't.
5   a   at a school   b   at a lab

8 **INTEGRATE** Write four questions to ask a classmate about his or her plans for the future.

9 **INTERACT** Ask and answer your questions from Exercise 8 with your partner. Share your
plans with the class.

1 ▶ **ACTIVATE** Watch the video. Answer the questions.

1 Who makes an invitation?
2 What is the invitation for?

2 **IDENTIFY** Complete the sentences about the video.

1 Kevin got a really big new ___TV_____.
2 People are going to watch _____ at his house on _____.
3 The game starts at _____.
4 _____ says "yes" to the invitation.
5 _____ can't go because he has a big, important _____
on Monday.
6 They are going to eat _____ at 8:30.

REAL-WORLD ENGLISH Accepting and refusing invitations

You can use these phrases to say *yes* to an invitation:

OK!
Yeah!
Sure!
Great, thanks!
That sounds great!
That sounds like fun!
I'd love to!

When you say *no*, use these phrases to show the other person that you're happy he or she invited you:

I'd (really) love to, but…
I'm sorry, I can't.
Sorry. I have plans (that day).
Thanks (for inviting me), but…
It sounds great, but I'm going to (be busy that day).

3 ▶ **INTEGRATE** Watch the video again. Which phrases from the box do Max and Andy use in the video?

ENGLISH FOR REAL

4 **ANALYZE** For each invitation, choose the more polite way to say *no*.

1 Invite: There's a really great play on Friday night. Would you like to go?
    Reply: a No, I don't have any money.
           b That sounds like fun, but I can't spend the money right now.

2 Invite: I'm going to have a party next Saturday. Can you come?
    Reply: a Oh, no! It sounds great, but I work on Saturday.
           b No, I can't. I work on Saturdays.

3 Invite: Sam and I are going to go out for pizza tonight. Come with us!
    Reply: a I don't want to go out tonight.
           b I'm sorry, but I'm busy tonight!

4 Invite: If you're free, I'm going to have some friends over for dinner on Sunday.
    Reply: a I'd love to, but I have plans on Sunday.
           b I'm not free. I have plans.

5 Invite: Do you want to go to the football game with me tomorrow?
    Reply: a No, I don't like football.
           b Thanks, but I'm not really a big football fan.

5 **IDENTIFY** Read through the scenarios. Think about phrases you can use to make and reply to the invitations.

Scenario 1: Student A: You're going to have a birthday party at your house next Saturday. Invite Student B.

           Student B: You don't have plans next Saturday and would really like to do something fun.

Scenario 2: Student A: Invite Student B to go for coffee with you after class.

           Student B: You are very busy today!

Scenario 3: Student A: You're going to go to a museum next weekend. Maybe Student B wants to go with you.

           Student B: You really love museums and you're not going to be busy next weekend.

Scenario 4: Student A: You bought tickets to a popular movie on Friday, but your friend can't go. Invite Student B.

           Student B: You don't have plans on Friday night, but you aren't interested in this movie.

6 **INTERACT** Choose one scenario and role-play with a partner. Then choose another scenario and switch roles.

7 **IMPROVE** Watch and listen to another pair's conversation. Give them feedback. Did they use correct phrases for accepting and refusing invitations?

GO ONLINE
to create your own version
of the English For Real video.

1 **ACTIVATE** Listen to the people's plans for the weekend. Mark each activity on the card when you hear it. When you have three activities in a row (across, down, or diagonal), shout, "Bingo!"

ACTIVITY BINGO

travel	cook for friends	see a movie	visit parents
do homework	go to a party	meet friends	go to a museum
make a cake	clean the house	exercise at the gym	have a party

 SPEAKING Describing plans

Use *be + going to + infinitive* to talk about plans for the future. Include time expressions to tell people when your plans are.
On Saturday, I'm going to go to the art museum.

2 **PREPARE** Make your own bingo card. Use your own ideas for activities.

PRONUNCIATION SKILL Weak form of *going to*

When we use *going to* + verb to talk about future plans, it often sounds like "gonna."
*I'm **going to** clean the house. (Sounds like: I'm **gonna** clean the house.)*

3 **NOTICE** Listen. Which do you hear? Then listen again and repeat.

1	Are you going to study this weekend?	going to	gonna
2	We're going to have a party.	going to	gonna
3	I'm going to go to Chicago on Saturday.	going to	gonna
4	My mother is going to visit me tomorrow.	going to	gonna
5	She's going to stay home on Sunday.	going to	gonna

4 **WHAT'S YOUR ANGLE?** Make a list of activities you are going to do next weekend. Say when you are going to do each one.

5 **INTERACT** Share your plans for next weekend with the class. Use your list from Exercise 4. As you listen to your classmates' plans, play bingo using your card from Exercise 2.

Unit Reviews

Unit 1

VOCABULARY

1 Unscramble the letters to make job names.

1 crateeh   t_____
2 verrid   d_____
3 cosrec yaperl   s_____
4 numiicas   m_____
5 snubsnamowise   b_____

2 Complete the sentences with the correct countries or nationalities.

1 A Peruvian person is from _____.
2 An Italian person is from _____.
3 A French person is from _____.
4 A _____ person is from Mexico.
5 A _____ person is from the United Kingdom.

3 Match the numbers.

1 twenty   a   9
2 twelve   b   8
3 eighteen   c   12
4 eleven   d   2
5 six   e   18
6 eight   f   10
7 two   g   20
8 ten   h   11
9 seven   i   7
10 nine   j   6

 GO ONLINE to play the vocabulary game.

GRAMMAR

4 Complete the sentences with *am*, *is* or *are*.

1 Soo-Hyun _____ from South Korea.
2 Australia _____ a country.
3 I _____ a student.
4 My friends and I _____ good students.
5 Elias and Georgia _____ from Greece.
6 You _____ a teacher.
7 Alicia _____ a musician.

5 Rewrite the sentences from Exercise 4 using subject pronouns and short forms.

He's from South Korea.

6 Write negative short answers to the questions.

1 Is Tony a driver? _No, he isn't._
2 Is Jessica a soccer player? _____
3 Is India in the Middle East? _____
4 Are you a famous artist? _____
5 Are Spain and Portugal in Asia? _____
6 Are your friends musicians? _____

7 Work with a partner. Choose a person that your partner knows. Your partner asks questions about the person. Can your partner guess who it is? Switch roles.

A: Is the person a woman?
B: No, he isn't.
A: Is he…?

 GO ONLINE to play the grammar game.

DISCUSSION POINT

8 Read the quote. What does it mean? Write a quote that describes you. Share your quote with the class.

"I am not a number, I am a free man!"

—Number Six, *The Prisoner* (TV series 1967-68), selected from *Oxford Essential Quotations*, 5th ed., edited by Susan Ratcliffe

 GO ONLINE and listen to a podcast. Then add your comments to the discussion board.

ZOOM IN

9 What about you?

Task 1 Talk about yourself—your nationality, your job, where you are from.

Task 2 Write three sentences about a person you know.

Task 3 Find an image of someone doing a job (e.g., a musician, a doctor, a teacher). Tell the class about the person.

10 Complete the table.

	I did this well	I need more practice
Task 1		
Task 2		
Task 3		

Unit 2

VOCABULARY

1 Unscramble the letters to make the names of common things.

1 yesk _____
2 epitruc _____
3 promctue _____
4 legsssa _____
5 noyem _____

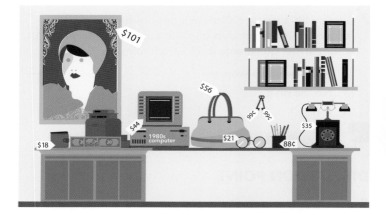

2 Write the numbers in words.

1 The picture is _one hundred and one_ dollars.
2 The pens are _____ cents each.
3 The keys are _____ cents each.
4 The large bag is _____ dollars.
5 The old phone is _____ dollars.
6 The glasses are _____ dollars.

 GO ONLINE to play the vocabulary game.

GRAMMAR

3 Complete the sentences with the correct words.

1 These are _good_ apples. (good / an)
2 _____ are popular animals. (Cat / Cats)
3 _____ people are famous. (A / Those)
4 Here's an _____. (gift / orange)
5 It's an _____ pen. (new / expensive)
6 Those are interesting _____. (book / books)

4 Choose the correct word.

1 *Brian / Brian's* children are Zoe and Nate.
2 *He / His* house is big.
3 *My / I* glasses are old.
4 *Maya / Maya's* friends are nice.
5 *Her / She* brother is a musician.
6 *We / Our* coffee shop is popular.

5 Write *this*, *that*, *these*, or *those*.

1 Is _this_ Mike's key? (near)
2 Are _____ your friends from Paris? (far)
3 _____ city is beautiful! (far)
4 _____ pens are all blue, not black. (near)
5 Paul, _____ is my friend Junko. (near)
6 Is _____ your notebook? (far)

 GO ONLINE to play the grammar game.

DISCUSSION POINT

6  Read the quote. Is it true for you? Are the best things in life free? What are some examples?

*"The moon belongs to everyone,
The best things in life are free,
The stars belong to everyone,
They gleam there for you
and me."*

—*"The Best Things in Life Are Free" (1927 song)*, selected from the *Oxford Dictionary of Modern Quotations*, 3rd ed., edited by Elizabeth Knowles

 GO ONLINE and listen to a podcast. Then add your comments to the discussion board.

ZOOM IN

7 What about you?

Task 1 Talk about two of your favorite things. What are they? Describe them.

Task 2 Imagine you have three gifts for three people. What are the gifts and who are they for? Write sentences.

Task 3 Bring in some items (or take a picture of them) that are important to you. Show them to your partner and describe them.

8 Complete the table.

	I did this well	I need more practice
Task 1		
Task 2		
Task 3		

Unit 3

VOCABULARY

1 Look at the images. Where can we find these things?

at a museum	~~in a bank~~	at an airport	in a park
in a store	in a café	in a supermarket	in a hotel

1 _in a bank_   5 _____
2 _____   6 _____
3 _____   7 _____
4 _____   8 _____

2 Complete the paragraph with *in*, *on*, *between*, or *near*.

We are ¹_____ Toronto, Canada, this
week. Our hotel is ²_____ Spadina Avenue
³_____ Chinatown. There's a great
Chinese restaurant ⁴_____ the hotel.
It's ⁵_____ Dundas Street. Our hotel is also
⁶_____ the train station. There are two beautiful
theaters ⁷_____ our hotel and the train station.
There are many things to do ⁸_____ this city!

 GO ONLINE to play the vocabulary game.

GRAMMAR

3 Complete the commands.

Go	Don't go	Take	Turn	Eat

1 _____ at Joe's Restaurant.
2 _____ to that café. It's too expensive!
3 The train station isn't near here. _____ a taxi.
4 _____ straight down Bristol Avenue.
5 _____ right onto Main Street.

4 Make true sentences. Use *is*, *isn't*, *are*, or *aren't*.

1 There _____ any tall buildings in a small town.
2 There _____ planes at an airport.
3 There _____ a bedroom in a train station.
4 There _____ any cars in a bank.
5 There _____ bathrooms in a hotel.

5 Use the prompts to write *yes/no* questions.

1 a park / anywhere
   Is there a park anywhere?
2 any good restaurants / near the beach
   _____
3 a nice café / in the town center
   _____
4 any interesting museums / in the city
   _____
5 a bank / near here
   _____
6 a cheap hotel / near the train station
   _____

 GO ONLINE to play the grammar game.

DISCUSSION POINT

6 Read the quote. What does it mean? Is it true for you?

"Home, sweet home."

—title of song from *"Clari, or, The Maid of Milan"* (1823 opera),
selected from *Oxford Essential Quotations,* 5ᵗʰ ed., edited by
Susan Ratcliffe

 **GO ONLINE and listen to a podcast. Then add
your comments to the discussion board.**

ZOOM IN

7 What about you?

Task 1 Talk about a place near the school. Say what the
place is and why it's interesting. Give directions
from the school.

Task 2 Write a review (3–4 sentences) of a hotel or other
public building you know. Describe the location,
the rooms, and interesting places nearby.

Task 3 Find an image of a city. Show the class. Describe
and point to some interesting things about the city.

8 Complete the table.

	I did this well	I need more practice
Task 1		
Task 2		
Task 3		

Unit 4

VOCABULARY

1 Write the days of the week.

1 M_____
2 _____
3 W_____
4 _____
5 _____
6 S_____
7 _____

2 Look at the image. Answer the questions.

1 Who is Leslie's husband? _____
2 Who are Ben's sons? _____
3 Who is Matt's sister? _____
4 Who are Alicia's parents? _____
5 Who is Ryan's brother? _____
6 Who is Ryan's mother? _____

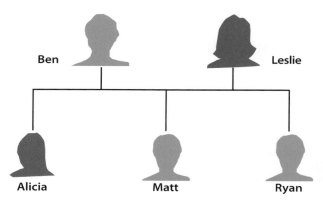

Ben   Leslie

Alicia   Matt   Ryan

 GO ONLINE to play the vocabulary game.

GRAMMAR

3 Read the text. Find the verbs in the simple present. There are 10.

Maggie is a nurse. She works at a hospital in the city. She goes to work in the evenings on Mondays, Tuesdays, and Wednesdays. She starts at 9 p.m., eats at 2 a.m., and finishes at 9 a.m. She doesn't go to work on the other days. She has four days off. She sleeps on Thursdays and does fun things on Fridays, Saturdays, and Sundays.

4 Choose the correct word.

1 I *don't* / *doesn't* have brothers or sisters.
2 Maria doesn't *have* / *has* time to go to the gym.
3 My son is four years old. He *don't* / *doesn't* go to school.
4 We don't *work* / *works* on weekends.
5 My father doesn't *do* / *does* fun things.
6 Bai and Chenhua *don't* / *doesn't* live in Beijing now.

5 Put the words in order to make questions.

1 you / spend / family / do / with / your / time ?
_____

2 do / homework / she / on / nights / does / Sunday ?
_____

3 I / do / good / make / coffee ?
_____

4 they / early / get / do / up ?
_____

5 do / go / to / ten / at / bed / you ?
_____

 GO ONLINE to play the grammar game.

DISCUSSION POINT

6 Read the quote. Is this true for you? Is your daily routine busy? Do you have time to do fun things?

"The less of routine, the more of life."

—Amos Bronson Alcott, selected from *Oxford Essential Quotations*, 5th ed., edited by Susan Ratcliffe

 GO ONLINE and listen to a podcast. Then add your comments to the discussion board.

ZOOM IN

7 What about you?

Task 1 Talk about two things you do and two things you don't do that help you to be happy.

Task 2 Write three sentences about what someone you know does every day.

Task 3 Find an image of your family or a famous family. Show the class and explain who's who in the picture.

8 Complete the table.

	I did this well	I need more practice
Task 1		
Task 2		
Task 3		

Unit 5

VOCABULARY

1 Complete the sentence with the correct form of the underlined word.

1 Seth is a _____. He <u>drives</u> for a ride-sharing service.

2 Xiao-Ling is a _____. She plays the <u>guitar</u>.

3 The O'Connors are _____. They work for the <u>science</u> department at the university.

4 Judy Balan is an Indian _____. She <u>writes</u> funny books and blogs.

5 We're _____. We're on a <u>tour</u> of Europe.

2 Match the sentence halves.

1 I don't usually fly   a subway into the city.

2 Many people learn to drive a

     b by train across the country.

     c boat from California to Japan.

3 I like to ride my

4 Keira often travels   d from that airport.

5 We usually take the   e bike on the bike path in the forest.

6 Jeff wants to sail his   f car at age 16.

 GO ONLINE to play the vocabulary game.

GRAMMAR

3 Choose the correct phrase to complete the sentence.

1 I do my homework every day. I _____ my homework.
   a do always   b always do   c sometimes do

2 We _____ to restaurants. They're expensive, and we like making dinner at home.
   a often go   b never go   c go never

3 Samantha doesn't _____ to work. She takes the subway.
   a usually drive   b drive usually   c never drive

4 The music _____ good on this radio station. I love it.
   a usually is   b is usually   c is never

5 I usually walk to class, but I _____ the bus because I'm late.
   a sometimes take   b often take   c usually take

4 Put the words in the correct order to make questions. Add punctuation. Then ask and answer the questions with a partner.

1 to / do / how / usually / get / you / work
   _____

2 why / people / take / subway / do / the
   _____

3 do / go / how / the / you / airport / to
   _____

4 tickets / I / how / buy / do / for / concert / a
   _____

5 ride-sharing / what / app / you / do / use
   _____

 GO ONLINE to play the grammar game.

DISCUSSION POINT

5 Read the quote. Do you usually travel with friends, with family, or by yourself? Do you like traveling alone? Why?

"It is easier to find a travelling companion than to get rid of one."

—Peg Bracken, selected from *The Oxford Dictionary of Humorous Quotations*, 5th ed., edited by Gyles Brandreth

 GO ONLINE and listen to a podcast. Then add your comments to the discussion board.

ZOOM IN

6 What about you?

Task 1 Talk about something you love doing and something you hate doing. How often do you do these things?

Task 2 Write a paragraph describing how you travel to class, to work, and around town for fun.

Task 3 Find an image of a place you like visiting. Describe to the class why you like going there, how often you go, and how you get there.

7 Complete the table.

	I did this well	I need more practice
Task 1		
Task 2		
Task 3		

Unit 6

VOCABULARY

1 Complete the sentences. Use the vocabulary words from page 64.

1 We can't _____ things well at night.
2 Can you _____ Portuguese?
3 My brother can _____ superheroes well with his colored pencils.
4 I love music, but I can't _____ an instrument.
5 Can you _____ a photo of me with my family?
6 You can't _____ Mount Everest without help.

2 Unscramble the abilities. Write example sentences.

1 *aylp nensit* p_lay____ t_ennis_____
   I play tennis with my friends on Sundays.
2 *emmerbre* r_____ information
3 *alpy muctepro* p_____ c_____ games
4 *gins* s_____ songs
5 *antip* p_____ pictures
6 *mupj* j_____ high

3 Work in groups. Share your example sentences from Exercise 2. Who has the most interesting sentence?

4 Use the phrases and the prompts to write complete sentences.

good at   great at   bad at   terrible at

1 We understand everything our teacher says in class. (explaining) _She's great at explaining things._
2 Those girls play soccer and basketball. (sports)
   _____
3 Wow, are you an artist? (painting)
   _____
4 I can't sing or play an instrument. (music)
   _____
5 He speaks Turkish, Arabic, Farsi, and Urdu. (languages)
   _____

 GO ONLINE to play the vocabulary game.

GRAMMAR

5 Choose the correct word.

1 This song is *terrible / terribly*.
2 Claire can speak French *beautiful / beautifully*.
3 They are *great / greatly* tennis players.
4 Your pictures are *good / well*.
5 Pablo is an *excellent / excellently* climber.

6 Put the words in the correct order to form questions.

1 you / can / a / picture / nice / draw
   _____
2 play / piano / Vanya / can / the
   _____
3 students / the / remember / can / words / the
   _____
4 your / play / can / roommate / basketball
   _____
5 Spanish / speak / I / well / can
   _____

 GO ONLINE to play the grammar game.

DISCUSSION POINT

7 ⊞ Read the quote. Which activity is Michael Phelps great at? Do you think it's important to be great at one thing or to be good at many things? What do you want to be great at?

"Eat, sleep and swim. That's all I can do."

—Michael Phelps, selected from *Oxford Essential Quotations*, 5th ed., edited by Susan Ratcliffe

GO ONLINE and listen to a podcast. Then add your comments to the discussion board.

ZOOM IN

8 What about you?

Task 1 Find someone who can do something you can't. Ask the person questions about the ability.

Task 2 Write five sentences about a fun activity you can do really well. How often do you do it? Why do you like it?

Task 3 Find an image of a famous person. Describe his or her abilities using *can / can't*, *good / bad at* + noun, and adverbs.

9 Complete the table.

	I did this well	I need more practice
Task 1		
Task 2		
Task 3		

Unit 7

VOCABULARY

1 Write the dates in words.

1 5/18 <u>May eighteenth</u>
2 7/24 _____
3 2/10 _____
4 4/11 _____
5 10/31 _____

2 Choose the logical answer.

1 It's dark today because of the *clouds / wind* in the sky.
2 We swim in the lake on *cold / hot* days.
3 We can't play soccer in the park now. There's a lot of *warm / rain* today.
4 I want to walk home because it's nice and *cool / cold* today.
5 We can't drive to the city now because of the *clouds / snow* on the streets.
6 The weather is great today! The *sun / hot* is out!

 GO ONLINE to play the vocabulary game.

GRAMMAR

3 Complete the sentences with *was, wasn't, were,* or *weren't*.

I stayed home on Saturday night because the weather ¹_____ bad. The streets ²_____ very dangerous. I ³_____ happy because I wanted to see my friends! My friends ⁴_____ at a fun Spanish restaurant in the city. They are roommates, and they live near the restaurant, so they ⁵_____ worried about the weather or the streets.

Sunday ⁶_____ a nice day. The weather ⁷_____ bad—in fact, it ⁸_____ beautiful! My friends and I ⁹_____ outside all day.

4 Put the words in the correct order to make questions. Add punctuation.

1 the / interesting / movie / was

   _____

2 you / where / on / Sunday / were

   _____

3 your / home / were / friends / yesterday

   _____

4 Saturday / wasn't / why / he / work / at / on

   _____

5 weren't / party / at / you / the / why

   _____

5 Write the simple past tense of the verb. Use the words in a sentence.

1 walk / home
   <u>We walked home after class because the</u>
   <u>weather was beautiful.</u>
2 arrive / airport _____
3 cook / breakfast _____
4 call / mother _____
5 students / talk _____
6 friend / play _____
7 answer / question _____

 GO ONLINE to play the grammar game.

DISCUSSION POINT

6 Read the quote. Do you agree? How can education help you to be successful?

"If you want to know the reason why I'm standing here, it's because of education. I never cut class."

—Michelle Obama, selected from *Oxford Essential Quotations*, 5ᵗʰ ed., edited by Susan Ratcliffe

 GO ONLINE and listen to a podcast. Then add your comments to the discussion board.

ZOOM IN

7 What about you?

Task 1 Where were you last Saturday? Why were you there? What was the weather like?

Task 2 Think about something bad you did to someone recently. Write a short email (three sentences) to apologize to the other person.

Task 3 Find a photo of an important event in your life. Share with the class. What happened, and what were the important dates?

8 Complete the table.

	I did this well	I need more practice
Task 1		
Task 2		
Task 3		

Unit 8

VOCABULARY

1 Complete the paragraph with the correct phrases.

in	in the	ago	last	on

My grandmother was born in Chile ¹_____ April 1, 1937.
She came to the United States ²_____ 1957. ³_____ late
1950s and early 1960s, she worked at an office in Houston.
Then she met and married my grandfather. They had
two children. My grandfather died ten years ⁴_____ at the
age of 74. My grandmother died ⁵_____ year. She was a
wonderful woman.

2 Describe each item of clothes. Include the color.

1 _a pair of blue jeans_   4 _____

2 _____   5 _____

3 _____   6 _____

> **GO ONLINE to play the vocabulary game.**

GRAMMAR

3 Complete the sentences with the past tense of the verb.

1 (spend) I _____ $80 on a new pair of jeans.
2 (have) King Henry VIII _____ six wives.
3 (write) Omar Khayyam _____ beautiful poems.
4 (buy) A new company _____ the Ritz Hotel from its original owners.
5 (think) We _____ it was a beautiful journey.
6 (make) The ancient Egyptians _____ paper from plants.
7 (take) We _____ the train across Europe last May.

4 Write *yes/no* questions in the simple past. Add punctuation.

1 people in Europe / eat chocolate in the 1400s
   Did Europeans eat chocolate in the 1400s?
2 the ancient Greeks / have cars
   _____
3 Mozart / write music
   _____
4 Cleopatra / live in Mexico
   _____
5 Marilyn Monroe / act in movies
   _____
6 people in China / drink tea 1,000 years ago
   _____

5 Work with a partner. Take turns asking the questions from Exercise 7. Give short answers.

> **GO ONLINE to play the grammar game.**

DISCUSSION POINT

6 Read the quote. Do you think the past is very different from the present? How?

"The past is a foreign country: they do things differently there."

—L. P. Hartley, selected from the *Oxford Dictionary of Quotations*, 8th ed., edited by Elizabeth Knowles

> **GO ONLINE and listen to a podcast. Then add your comments to the discussion board.**

ZOOM IN

7 What about you?

Task 1 Talk about last weekend. Describe two things you did and two things you didn't do.

Task 2 Imagine you can write to a person from history. Write three questions using the simple past.

Task 3 Find a photo from when you were a child. What year is the photo from? Tell your partner about the time when the photo was taken.

8 Complete the table.

	I did this well	I need more practice
Task 1		
Task 2		
Task 3		

Unit 9

VOCABULARY

1 Unscramble the words for food and drinks.

1 kilm _____   4 sgeg _____
2 sifh _____   5 ecir _____
3 tame _____   6 rifut _____

2 Label the furniture in the dorm room.

| desk | chair | refrigerator | bed | table | lamp | sofa | TV |

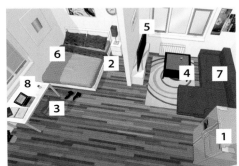

1 _____
2 _____
3 _____
4 _____
5 _____
6 _____
7 _____
8 _____

3 Match the related sentences.

1 I need to sleep.   a I'm tired.
2 I'd like to eat.   b It's open at 9:00.
3 I'd like to drink some water.   c I'm hungry.
4 I want to go to the market.   d I'm not ready.
5 We can't go to the library today.   e It's closed.
6 Wait for me. I need 15 minutes.   f I'm thirsty.

GO ONLINE to play the vocabulary game.

GRAMMAR

4 Is the underlined noun countable or uncountable?

1 Do you have any <u>children</u>?   _____
2 She has a lot of <u>friends</u>.   _____
3 I don't eat a lot of <u>fish</u>.   _____
4 Would you like some <u>rice</u>?   _____
5 Many <u>people</u> like this restaurant. _____
6 <u>Vegetables</u> are good for you.   _____

5 Write *much* or *many*.

1 How _____ water do you usually drink every day?
2 How _____ students are there in your class?
3 How _____ English homework do you do?
4 How _____ milk do you have in your tea?
5 How _____ books are on the table?

6 Work with a partner. Ask and answer the questions from Exercise 5.

7 Choose the correct answer.

1 I don't have _____ money.
   a some   b any   c many

2 I have _____ fruit.
   a some   b any   c many

3 There are _____ cars on the street.
   a any   b much   c many

4 The market sells _____ vegetables.
   a a lot   b much   c a lot of

5 There isn't _____ food on the table.
   a any   b many   c a lot

GO ONLINE to play the grammar game.

DISCUSSION POINT

8 Read the quote. Do you agree? In your opinion, what makes a house comfortable?

"A comfortable house is a great source of happiness."

—Sydney Smith, selected from *Oxford Essential Quotations*, 5th ed., edited by Susan Ratcliffe

GO ONLINE and listen to a podcast. Then add your comments to the discussion board.

ZOOM IN

9 What about you?

Task 1 Talk about your favorite restaurant. Why do you like it? What do you like to eat there? Invite a classmate to go there with you.

Task 2 Write three sentences about your home. Describe the furniture you have.

Task 3 Find a photo of a comfort food you made or ate. Tell your partner about it.

10 Complete the table.

	I did this well	I need more practice
Task 1		
Task 2		
Task 3		

Unit 10

VOCABULARY

1 Write the names of the places. Compare your answers with a partner.

1 This is a very dry, hot place. _____

2 This is a place in Scotland: The _____ of Cosmic Speculation.

3 It's a large body of water, like the Mediterranean or the Caribbean. _____

4 It's a body of water. It can be big or small. You can find one in the forest or in the mountains. _____

5 There are many trees and wild animals here. It's a good place for camping. _____

2 Choose the correct adjective.

1 I like to stay in *dark / interesting* hotels.

2 I love the desert. I think the colors are *pretty / scary*.

3 Bring warm clothes. The mountains are *cool / dark* at night.

4 We can't go in the forest at night. It's *safe / dangerous*.

5 It's *cool / warm* today. Let's go to the beach.

3 Complete the sentences with the correct words.

1 In December, I went on *vacation / suitcase* with a friend.

2 We took a *trip / break* to Costa Rica.

3 It was a perfect *winter / summer* vacation because it's always warm in Costa Rica.

4 I packed a big *break / suitcase* because we stayed for three weeks.

5 I can't take another big vacation this year, but I want to go on a short *break / summer* to visit my parents.

 GO ONLINE to play the vocabulary game.

GRAMMAR

4 Write the correct object pronoun.

1 My <u>parents</u> were interested in my trip, so I called ___them___ when I arrived.

2 Where are the cave <u>paintings</u>? I don't see _____.

3 We visited the <u>countryside</u> last weekend. I loved _____!

4 My <u>brother</u> lives in Trinidad. I visited _____ last month.

5 Do <u>you</u> want to see pictures from my vacation? I can show them to _____.

5 Choose the logical adjective. Then write the comparative form.

1 (green / red) A forest is _greener than_ a desert.

2 (busy / calm) A city is _____ the countryside.

3 (big / small) A city is _____ a village.

4 (wet / dry) A forest is _____ a desert.

5 (short / tall) Mountains are _____ hills.

6 (good / bad) Staying at a hotel is _____ camping outside in cold weather.

7 (expensive / cheap) The trip from England to Brazil is _____ the trip from England to Portugal.

 GO ONLINE to play the grammar game.

DISCUSSION POINT

6 Read the quote. Do you agree? Write your own quote following the same structure: "There is only one thing in the world worse than…, and that is…"

"There is only one thing in the world worse than being talked about, and that is not being talked about."

—Oscar Wilde, selected from *Oxford Essential Quotations*, 5th ed., edited by Susan Ratcliffe

 GO ONLINE and listen to a podcast. Then add your comments to the discussion board.

ZOOM IN

7 What about you?

Task 1 Talk about a good or a bad adventure. What happened?

Task 2 Choose a place in the world where you'd like to live. Write four sentences comparing it to the place you live now. Use comparative adjectives.

Task 3 Find images of two different types of places or things. Share with the class. Explain how they are different.

8 Complete the table.

	I did this well	I need more practice
Task 1		
Task 2		
Task 3		

Unit 11

VOCABULARY

1 Complete the paragraph with the correct words.

I ¹*take / learn* business classes at college, and we ²*try / learn* a lot about the business world. I work hard. I ³*do / take* notes in class, and I always ⁴*make / do* my homework. We ⁵*make / write* a lot of papers in this class.

2 Complete the sentences with the phrases.

learn new skills	works for a large company
helps people	looking for a new job
makes a lot of money	

1 Seth wants to be a chef, but he can't cook. He'd like to _____.

2 Amanda hates her job. She's _____.

3 Monica is a nurse. She _____.

4 Pedro is a computer programmer for Microsoft. He _____.

5 Mark lives in a big house and drives an expensive car. He _____.

3 Choose the logical ending for each sentence.

1 Taking notes in class and reading them later can help you *remember a lesson / move around*.

2 Sitting at your desk all day is not healthy. It's important to *understand / move*.

3 I don't understand what this word means. I need *a problem / an example*.

4 You don't understand how to do use the website? I can *show you / remember it*.

5 Working in a group makes it easier to work through *problems / skills*.

 GO ONLINE to play the vocabulary game.

GRAMMAR

4 Write present continuous sentences using the words.

1 the teacher / explain / a math problem
   The teacher's explaining a math problem.

2 the students / take / notes
   _____

3 she / learn / a new skill
   _____

4 they / write / messages
   _____

5 he / help / someone
   _____

6 she / do / well
   _____

5 Complete the questions with the correct verb forms in the present continuous.

1 (do) What _is_ he _doing_ ?

2 (live) Where _____ you _____ now?

3 (study) _____ she _____ Arabic?

4 (go) Where _____ we _____ now?

5 (run) Why _____ they _____ ?

6 Complete the sentences using the -*ing* form of the verb as the subject.

1 _Playing tennis_ is fun. (play tennis)

2 I think that _____ is very interesting. (learn)

3 _____ is dangerous. (ride a motorcycle)

4 For me, _____ is boring. (watch TV)

5 _____ is good exercise. (dance)

 GO ONLINE to play the grammar game.

DISCUSSION POINT

7 Read the quote. Do you agree? How can learning change the world?

"One child, one teacher, one book and one pen can change the world. Education is the only solution. Education first."

—Malala Yousafzai, selected from *Oxford Essential Quotations*, 5ᵗʰ ed., edited by Susan Ratcliffe

 GO ONLINE and listen to a podcast. Then add your comments to the discussion board.

ZOOM IN

8 What about you?

Task 1 Talk about a skill you're trying to learn. What are you doing to get better at it?

Task 2 Write three study tips for learning English. Use -*ing* forms as the subjects of your sentences.

Task 3 Find an image of someone doing something interesting. Describe what is happening.

9 Complete the table.

	I did this well	I need more practice
Task 1		
Task 2		
Task 3		

Unit 12

VOCABULARY

1 Unscramble the words. Then match them to the pictures.

| yodalhi | harbityd | kace | cie ramec | adnwhcseis | veinit |

  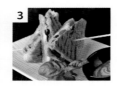

_____ _____ _____

_____ _____ _____

2 Choose all the correct options to complete the sentences.

1 I'm going to graduate next *hour / week / month*.
2 Are you going to be in class *tomorrow / later / now*?
3 My parents are going to travel to Madrid next *week / hour / day*.
4 They're going to leave in an *hour / today / tomorrow*.
5 We're going to go out this *morning / night / evening*.

 GO ONLINE to play the vocabulary game.

GRAMMAR

3 Complete the sentences about future plans.

1 (they / have) _They're going to have_ a dinner party on Friday.
2 (he / work) _____ as a waiter this summer.
3 (I / make) _____ sandwiches for the party tonight.
4 (she / buy) _____ an expensive cake.
5 (we / visit) _____ the Circus Maximus in Rome next month.

4 Put the words in order to make questions.

1 when / going / are / we / to / dinner / eat

_____

2 you / are / go / now / to / going / home

_____

3 on / what / going / are / to / you / do / Saturday

_____

4 is / a / going / she / have / to / party

_____

5 going / are / music / to / they / play

_____

6 he / is / going / to / where / travel

_____

5 Choose the correct word(s).

1 Next New Year's Eve I'm going to have the *bigger / biggest / big* party ever!
2 For my friend, making cakes is *more / the most / most* interesting activity.
3 Amazon is one of the most *popular / nicest / better* stores on the Internet.
4 For me, riding a bike in the city with lots of cars is the most *scariest / crazier / dangerous* activity.
5 For me, the *bad / worse / worst* thing is to get up early and go to work when I feel sick.

 GO ONLINE to play the grammar game.

DISCUSSION POINT

6 Read the quote. Are these the words of an optimist or a pessimist? Why do you think so?

"Cheer up! The worst is yet to come!"

—Philander Chase Johnson, selected from the *Oxford Dictionary of Quotations,* 8th ed., edited by Elizabeth Knowles

GO ONLINE and listen to a podcast. Then add your comments to the discussion board.

ZOOM IN

7 What about you?

Task 1 Talk about two things you're going to do in the future and why.

Task 2 Write three sentences using *be + going to* + infinitive to describe three of your goals for next year.

Task 3. Find an image of a sports event, concert, or party you went to. Use superlative adjectives to describe it.

8 Complete the table.

	I did this well	I need more practice
Task 1		
Task 2		
Task 3		

Grammar focus

Unit 1

Be: Positive and subject pronouns

FORM

Be is an irregular verb. *Be* is the infinitive. It has three different forms in the simple present tense.

Subject pronoun	*be*	
I	*am*	Sue.
You	*are*	here to study.
He/She/It	*is*	Spanish.
We/You/They	*are*	from Brazil.

> **Tip**
>
> We use short forms in spoken English.
>
> I am → I'm   You are → You're
> He is → He's   She is → She's   It is → It's
> We are → We're   They are → They're

USE

We can use *be* for name, age, nationality, and jobs.

I'm Anna. She's fifteen. We're from Poland.

Be: *Yes/no* questions and short answers

FORM

Yes/No questions (?)		
Be	**Subject**	
Am	I	a student? from Italy?
Are	you	
Is	he/she/it	
Are	we	students? from Italy?
Are	you	
Are	they	

Short answers	
Positive (+)	**Negative (−)**
Yes, I *am*.	No, I*'m not*.
Yes, you *are*.	No, you *aren't*. OR You*'re not*.
Yes, he/she/it *is*.	No, he/she/it *isn't*. OR He/She/It*'s not*.
Yes, we *are*.	No, we *aren't*. OR We*'re not*.
Yes, you *are*.	No, you *aren't*. OR You*'re not*.
Yes, they *are*.	No, they *aren't*. OR They*'re not*.

USE

We use *be* to ask about name, age, nationality, and jobs.

"Is she a doctor?"   "Yes, she is."

Be: *Wh-* questions

FORM

Question word	*be*	subject	
What	*is*	your name?	
Where	*are*	you	from?
Who	*is*	your teacher?	
When	*is*	the class?	
Why	*are*	you	happy?
How old	*are*	you?	

USE

We use *be* with question words to ask about name, age and nationality.

Be: Negative

FORM

Subject pronoun	*be*	*not*	
I	*am*	*not*	French.
You	*are*		a teacher.
He She It	*is*		Max. Sarah. Tuesday.
We You They	*are*		doctors. students. from Italy.

> **Tip**
>
> We use short forms in spoken English.
>
> I am not → I'm not. (NOT I amn't.)
> You are not → You *aren't*/You*'re not*
> He is not → He *isn't*/He's *not*
> She is not → She *isn't*/She's *not*
> It is not → It *isn't*/It's *not*
> We are not → We *aren't*/We*'re not*
> They are not → They *aren't*/They*'re not*

 GO ONLINE for the complete grammar reference.

Unit 2

Nouns: Singular and plural

Most nouns have a singular form and a plural form.

a/an + singular noun

We use *an* with singular nouns that start with a vowel.

an apple (NOT ~~a apple~~)

For most plural nouns, add *-s*.

apple → apple*s*   banana → banana*s*

Tip

Add *-es* after *-x*, *-sh*, *-ss*, *-ch* and sometimes after *-o*.

box → box*es*   dish → dish*es*   kiss → kiss*es*

beach → beach*es*   tomato → tomato*es*

Change *-y* to *-ies*.

party → part*ies*

Some plural nouns are irregular. We don't form the plural with
-s or *-es*.

some women/men (NOT ~~some womans/mens~~)

three children (NOT ~~three childs~~)

a lot of people (NOT ~~a lot of persons~~)

Demonstrative adjectives and pronouns: *This, that, these, those*

We use demonstrative adjectives *this* or *these* with nouns to
talk about people or things that are near us. They go before the
noun.

This chair's comfortable.   *These cups are dirty.*

We use demonstrative adjectives *that* or *those* with nouns to
talk about people or things that aren't near us.

That cafe's open.

"Where are those people from?" "They're from Spain."

We use demonstrative pronouns *this* or *these* with *is/are* to talk
about things or people that are near us.

This is my phone.

These are my friends.

We use demonstrative pronouns *that* or *those* with *is/are* to talk
about things or people that aren't near us.

That's her phone.

Those are my shoes.

Possessive *'s*

FORM

Name + *'s*	noun
Maya*'s*	coat
Sarah*'s*	books

USE

We use possessive *'s* to talk about things or people that belong
to a person, place or thing.

We use *'s* to talk about possessions with names.

It's Maya's coat.   *They are Tom's friends.*

We use possessive *'s* with names or words that end with *s*.

Where is Ross's bag?

We can use possessive *'s* with a possessive adjective and noun.

This is my father's phone.

We add *'* (not *'s*) to a plural noun that ends with *s*.

This is my parents' house. (NOT ~~This is my parents's house.~~)

Possessive adjectives

FORM

Subject pronoun	Possessive adjective
I'm Spanish.	*My* family is from Miami.
You're tall.	*Your* sister is tall.
He's a student.	*His* name is Max.
She's an artist.	*Her* paintings are good.
It's a good hotel.	*Its* rooms are big.
We're students.	*Our* school is new.
You're friends.	*Your* brothers are friends.
They're sisters.	*Their* parents are old.

USE

We use possessive adjectives with a noun to show that
something belongs to somebody.

We use possessive adjectives to talk about possessions.

Our house is messy.

We use possessive adjectives to talk about family and friends.

My family is from Miami.

We use possessive adjectives to talk about appearance.

Her eyes are blue.

 GO ONLINE for the complete grammar reference.

Unit 3

There is …/There are …

FORM

	Singular	Plural
Positive (+)	*There's an* airport.	*There are some* restaurants.
Negative (–)	*There isn't a* hotel.	*There aren't any* museums.
Questions (?)	*Is there a* railway station?	*Are there any* stores?
Short answers	Yes, there is. No, there isn't.	Yes, there are. No, there aren't.

USE

We use *There is / There are* to talk about things that are in a place.

> *In my town there's a river.*
> *There are some books on the table.*

We use *a/an* with singular countable nouns.

> *There's a museum, but there isn't a lake.*

We also use *There is* with the number *one*.

> *There's only one cookie – it's for you!*

We use *There are + some* or a number with plural countable nouns.

> *There are two farms near us.*

> **Tip**
> In a list of things, we use *There is* if the first word is singular and *There are* if the first word is plural.
>
> > *In the hotel, there is a swimming pool, a store, and sixty rooms.*
> > *There are some restaurants, a bar, and an old church.*

There is …/There are …: Negative and questions

> **Tip**
> We often use short forms.
>
> > There is not → There *isn't*
> > There are not → There *aren't*

USE

We use *There aren't any* with plural countable nouns in negative sentences.

> *There aren't any mountains here.*

We use *Is there…? / Are there …?* to ask about things in a place. We usually answer *yes/no* questions with short answers. We use *a/an* with singular countable nouns in questions.

> "*Is there a beach?*" "*No, there isn't.*"

We use *any* before plural nouns in questions.

> "*Are there any flowers in your yard?*" "*Yes, there are.*"

We can use *There aren't many* with plural nouns to say there are fewer than we expect.

> *There aren't many tables in the restaurant.*

Imperatives

FORM

We form positive imperatives with the verb.

Positive (+)	
Verb	
Run!	
Throw	the ball!

We form negative imperatives with *Don't* + verb!

Negative (–)		
Don't	**verb**	
Don't	*run*!	
	throw	the ball!

We usually use the short form (*Don't*), but we sometimes use the full form (*Do not*) in formal writing.

USE

We use imperatives to say what we want someone to do.

> *Run!*   *Throw the ball!*

We use *Don't* + verb! to say what we don't want someone to do.

> *Don't run!*   *Don't throw the ball!*

We use the verb *be* with adjectives.

> *Be quiet!*   *Don't be late!*

We can use *have* with some nouns.

> *Have fun!*   *Have a nice day!*

 GO ONLINE for the complete grammar reference.

Unit 4

Simple present: Positive

FORM

Subject	verb	
I You	*teach*	at the university.
He/She It	*starts*	work at 7 a.m. at 7 p.m.
We You They	*live*	in Abu Dhabi.

USE

We use the simple present to talk about our lives and things we do every day/week, etc.

*I **live** in Cape Town.*

*I **get up** at six o'clock.*

We use the simple present to talk about facts, things that don't change.

*The President **lives** in the White House.*

We also use the simple present to talk about feelings and opinions.

*We **like** French movies.*

We use the simple present with *have* to talk about some actions.

*I **have** breakfast at seven o'clock.*

Simple present: *Yes/no* questions and short answers

FORM

We form *yes/no* questions in the simple present with:

Do/Does + subject + verb?

Yes/no questions (?)			
Do/Does	subject	verb	
Do	I you	go speak know like	to concerts? Italian? Mike? football?
Does	he/she/it		
Do	we you they		

We form short answers with:

Yes + subject + do/does.

No + subject + don't/doesn't.

Short answers			
Positive (+)		**Negative** (−)	
Yes, I Yes, you	*do.*	No, I No, you	*don't.*
Yes, he/she/it	*does.*	No, he/she/it	*doesn't.*
Yes, we Yes, you Yes, they	*do.*	No, we No, you No, they	*don't.*

USE

We use simple present questions to ask about people's lives and things we do every day/week, etc. We usually answer with a short answer.

*"**Do you** live in an apartment?"   "Yes, **I do**."*

We also use the simple present to ask about feelings, opinions and facts.

*"**Do the teachers** speak Polish?"   "No, **they don't**."*

Simple present: Negative

FORM

We form the simple present negative with:

Subject + don't/doesn't + verb.

Subject	don't/doesn't	verb	
I You	*don't*	teach walk speak drive like watch	math. to school. French. to work. football. TV.
He/She/It	*doesn't*		
We You They	*don't*		

USE

We use the simple present negative to talk about our lives and things we do every day/week, etc.

*We **don't live** in Rome.*

We also use the simple present negative to talk about feelings and opinions.

*I **don't like** pizza.*

We use the simple present negative to talk about facts and things that don't change.

*She **doesn't speak** French.*

 GO ONLINE for the complete grammar reference.

Unit 5

Adverbs: *Always, usually, often, sometimes,* and *never*

FORM

Positive (+)			
Subject	**adverb**	**verb**	
I	always usually often sometimes never	get up	early.

Negative (–)				
Subject	***don't/ doesn't***	**adverb**	**infinitive without to**	
I	*don't*	always usually often	have	breakfast.
You	*don't*			
He/She/It	*doesn't*			
We/You/ They	*don't*			

USE

We use adverbs of frequency with the simple present to say how often we do something.

100%				0%
always	usually	often	sometimes	never

We usually put the adverb between the subject and the verb.

> Andy **never gets up** before eight o'clock.

With the verb *be*, the adverb comes *after* the verb.

> Karen **is often** at home on Saturdays.

We don't use a negative verb with *never*.

> It **never rains**. (NOT It doesn't never rain.)

Like/love/hate + -ing forms

FORM

We can use the *ing*-form of a verb as a noun. It can be the object or subject of the verb.

Subject	**verb**	***ing*-form (object)**
I You	like don't like	singing. dancing. running. swimming. reading. painting.
He/She/It	enjoys doesn't enjoy	
We You They	love hate don't like	

Do/Does	**subject**	**verb**	***ing*-form (object)**
Do	I/you	like enjoy	going out? swimming? reading?
Does	he/she/it		
Do	we/you/they		

Tip			
Spelling rules			
Most verbs	add *-ing*	read → read*ing* sing → sing*ing*	
Verbs that end in *-e*	remove the *e* and add *-ing*	dance → danc*ing* ride → rid*ing*	
Verbs that end in vowel + consonant	double the consonant and add *-ing*	run → ru*nning* swim → swi*mming*	

USE

We use the *ing*-form in *wh*- questions to ask general questions.

> "What do you like **doing** in your free time?"   "I love **swimming**."

We use the *ing*-form in *yes/no* questions to ask about activities that we like/don't like. We often reply with a short answer.

> "Do you enjoy **running**?"   "Yes, I do."

Simple present: *Wh*- questions

FORM

Question word	***do/does***	**subject**	**verb**	
What	*do*	I	*need?*	
Where		you	*live?*	
When	*does*	the class	*start?*	
What time	*do*	we	*get up?*	
How		you	*get*	to school?
Why		they	*like*	football?

USE

We use different question words to ask about different types of information.

Question word	Information
What	things and activities
Who	people
When/What time	time
Where	places
How	way/manner
Why	reasons

 GO ONLINE for the complete grammar reference.

Unit 6

Can and *can't*

FORM

We use a verb after *can* and *can't*.

Subject + can/can't + verb.

Positive (+)			
Subject	*can*	**verb**	
I	can	swim.	
Negative (−)			
Subject	*can't*	**verb**	
They	can't	play	football.

Can't is the short form of *cannot*.

USE

We use *can* to talk about things we can do. We use *can't* to talk about things we can't do.

> *I can dance, but I can't sing.*

Can: *Yes/no* questions and short answers

FORM

To make questions with *can*, we change the order of the subject and *can*.

Can + subject + verb?

Questions (?)			
Can	**subject**	**verb**	
Can	you	play	the piano?

Short answers			
Positive (+)		**Negative** (−)	
Yes, I	*can*.	No, I	*can't*.

USE

We use *can* to ask if someone can do something.

We usually answer *yes/no* questions with short answers.

> *"**Can** they **swim**?"   "No, they **can't**."*

Adverbs of manner

FORM

We form most adverbs by adding *-ly* to the adjective.

Adverbs of manner		
most adjectives	add *-ly*	bad → bad*ly* quiet → quiet*ly*
adjective ends in *-y*	change *-y* to *-ily*	easy → eas*ily* happy → happ*ily*

Some adverbs are irregular and don't end in *–ly*. You have to learn these.

> good → *well*   fast → *fast*

USE

We use adverbs of manner to talk about how we do things.

> *Tom talks **quietly**.*
>
> *Jenna runs **fast**.*

GO ONLINE for the complete grammar reference.

Unit 7

Simple past of *be*: Positive and negative

FORM

Was and *wasn't* (*was not*) are the past forms of *is, isn't, am*
and *am not*. *Were* and *weren't* (*were not*) are the past forms of
are and *aren't*.

Positive (+)		
Subject	***was/were***	
I	*was*	happy then.
You	*were*	a teacher.
He/She/It	*was*	in class yesterday.
We/You/They	*were*	

Negative (−)		
Subject	***wasn't/weren't***	
I	*wasn't*	cold in the park.
You	*weren't*	rich.
He/She/It	*wasn't*	at home last night.
We/You/They	*weren't*	

USE

We often use *was/were* with past time expressions, e.g. *last
week, in 2003, 500 years ago, yesterday.*

> We **were** in Paris last week.

Simple past with *be*: Yes/no questions

FORM

We form *yes/no* questions with *be* in the simple past with:
Was/Were + subject (I, you, he, etc.) …?

Yes/no questions (?)		
Was/Were	**subject**	
Was	I	at home yesterday?
Were	you	
Was	he/she/it	
Were	we/you/they	

Short answers			
Positive (+)		**Negative (−)**	
Yes, I	*was.*	No, I	*wasn't.*
Yes, you	*were.*	No, you	*weren't.*
Yes, he/she/it	*was.*	No, he/she/it	*wasn't.*
Yes, we/you/they	*were.*	No, we/you/they	*weren't.*

USE

When we answer *yes/no* questions about the past, we usually
use short answers.

> "**Was** he friendly?"   "No, **he wasn't**."
> "**Was** there a cafe in your school?"   "Yes, **there was**."
> "**Were** Jenna and Karen in class yesterday?"   "Yes, **they were**."

Simple past with *be*: Wh- questions

FORM

We form *wh-* questions with *be* in the simple past with:
Question word + was/were + subject (I, you, he, etc.) …?

Wh- questions (?)			
Question word	***was/were***	**subject**	
What	*was*	your last job?	
Why	*was*	she	in Spain last week?
When	*were*	they	born?

USE

We often use *was/were* with past time expressions.

> "**Where were you** last week?"   "I was sick all week."

Simple past of regular verbs: Positive

FORM

We add *-ed* to form the simple past of regular verbs. The form
of the simple past is the same for every subject (*I, you, he*, etc.).

> I **played** football.   They **listened** to the radio.

Tip

Spelling rules: regular verbs		
	Simple past form	
most verbs	add *-ed*	play → play*ed*
ends in *-e*	add *-d*	live → live*d*
ends in a consonant + *-y*	change *-y* to *-ied*	study → stud*ied*
ends in one vowel + one consonant (except *w* and *y*)	double the consonant and add *-ed*	stop → stop*ped*

USE

When we use the simple past, we often say when the action
happened, e.g. *last winter, in 1999, for three days.*

> They **lived** in Egypt in 2005.

 GO ONLINE for the complete grammar reference.

Unit 8

Simple past of irregular verbs

FORM

With irregular verbs, we do not add -ed for the simple past form. There are no rules. They all have different forms.

Regular	
play → play*ed*	carry → carr*ied*
Irregular	
come → *came*	do → *did*
go → *went*	have → *had*
meet → *met*	see → *saw*

The simple past is the same for every subject (*I, you, he,* etc.) for both regular and irregular verbs, except for the verb *be*.

USE

We use the simple past to talk about finished actions and states in the past.

> *I **met** Dave in the park.*

When we use the simple past, we often say when the action happened, e.g. *last winter, in 1999, nine months ago, for three days*.

> *He **came** home at ten o'clock.*

Simple past: Negative

FORM

We form the simple past negative with *didn't*.

Subject (I, you, he, etc.) + didn't + verb.

Negative (–)			
Subject	***didn't***	**infinitive without to**	
I	*didn't*	have	breakfast.
You		watch	the movie.

We usually use the short form (*didn't*), but we sometimes use the full form (*did not*) in formal writing.

USE

We use the simple past to talk about finished actions and states in the past.

> *I **didn't have** breakfast this morning.*

Simple past: *Yes/no* questions

FORM

We form simple past *yes/no* questions with:

Did + subject + verb?

Yes/no questions (?)			
Did	**subject**	**verb**	
Did	I	arrive	on time?
	you	have	a good time?
	he/she/it	swim	in the ocean?
	we	meet	any interesting people?
	you		
	they		

The form is the same for every subject (*I, you, he,* etc.).
Notice that the main part of the structure is *arrive*, *swim*, etc., not the simple past form *arrived*, *swam*, etc.

> *Did they **arrive** on time?* (NOT ~~Did they arrived on time?~~)

Short answers			
Positive (+)		**Negative (–)**	
Yes, I	*did.*	No, I	*didn't.*
Yes, you		No, you	
Yes, he/she/it		No, he/she/it	
Yes, we		No, we	
Yes, you		No, you	
Yes, they		No, they	

USE

We use the questions in the simple past to ask about finished actions and states in the past. We often use it with past time expressions, e.g. *last week, in 2003, 500 years ago, yesterday*.

> *"**Did** you **go** on vacation last summer?"   "Yes, **I did**."*

GO ONLINE for the complete grammar reference.

Unit 9

Countable and uncountable nouns

FORM

Countable nouns have a singular form and a plural form.

a/an + singular countable noun

We use *some* with plural countable nouns in positive sentences.

We use *any* with plural countable nouns in negative sentences.

Plural		some /any	noun
+	I have	**some**	bananas.
–	I don't have	**any**	apples.

Uncountable nouns have no plural form.

singular	plural
bread	–
milk	–

We can use *some* + uncountable noun in positive sentences.

We can use *any* + uncountable noun in negative sentences.

		some/any	uncountable noun
+	I have	**some**	bread.
–	I don't have	**any**	milk.

USE

Countable nouns are things and people that we can count.

> I have **an apple** and **a banana**.

We use numbers with countable nouns to say how many.

> I eat **five vegetables** every day.

We can't count uncountable nouns.

> **some milk** (NOT ~~a milk~~ or ~~two milks~~)

Quantifiers: *Much/many/a lot of*

FORM

		Countable	Uncountable
+	I have	*a lot of/lots of* books.	*a lot of/lots of* time.
–	She doesn't eat	*many* apples.	*much* meat.

Countable		
How many potatoes are there?	A lot./Lots.	There are *a lot of/lots of* potatoes.
	Not many.	There are**n't** *many* potatoes.
	None.	There are**n't** *any* potatoes.

Uncountable		
How much cheese do you eat?	A lot./Lots.	I eat *a lot of/lots of* cheese.
	Not much.	I do**n't** eat **much** cheese.
	None.	I do**n't** eat **any** cheese.

USE

In positive sentences, we use *a lot of/lots of* with countable or uncountable nouns to talk about a big quantity of something.

> I drink *a lot of* milk.

In negative sentences, we use *much* with uncountable nouns, and *many* with countable nouns.

> I don't have **much** money. (= I have a small amount.)

We can also use *a lot of/lots of* in negative sentences with countable or uncountable nouns.

> I don't have *a lot of* time.

We use *How many* with countable nouns.

> **How many books** does she have?

We use *How much* with uncountable nouns.

> **How much cheese** do you eat?

We can answer with a short answer.

> "**How many stores** are there?" "**A few./ A lot.**"

We can answer with a sentence, using a quantifier + noun.

> "**How much money** do you have?" "I don't have **any money**."

Would like: Requests and offers

FORM

'd like is the same for every subject.

Subject + 'd like + noun/verb.

> You**'d like** some cake.

> They**'d like** to watch TV.

'd like is short for *would like*.

> We **would like** three tickets, please.

For questions, change the order of *would* and the subject.

Would + subject + like + noun/verb?

> **Would** you **like** a new coat?

Wh- questions				
Question word	*would*	subject	*like*	verb
What	*would*	you	*like*	to eat?

USE

We use *'d like* or *would like* to ask for something. It is a polite way of saying *want*. We use *would like* in formal writing.

> I**'d like** coffee and Cathy **would like** tea.

 GO ONLINE for the complete grammar reference.

167

Unit 10

Object pronouns

FORM

Subject pronoun	Object pronoun
I	*me*
you	*you*
he	*him*
she	*her*
it	*it*
we	*us*
you	*you*
they	*them*

USE

We use pronouns in place of nouns. The object pronoun goes after a verb.

> He likes **her**.

The object pronoun also goes after a preposition.

> He played a song **for us**.
>
> I'm studying English **with him**.

We use an object pronoun, not a subject pronoun, after the verb *be*.

> "Who's there?"   "It's **me** – Kate."

Comparative adjectives

FORM

For short adjectives, we usually form the comparative with *-er*.

Short **comparative adjectives**	
add *-er* or *-r*	tall → tall*er* long → long*er* nice → nic*er*
double the consonant and add *-er*	big → big*ger* hot → hot*ter*
change *-y* to *-ier*	happy → happ*ier* easy → eas*ier*

USE

We use comparative adjectives to describe how one thing or person is different from another thing or person.
We use comparative adjectives with *than*.

> Jack is **older than** Maya.
>
> Math is **easier than** physics.

When it is clear what we are talking about, we don't need to give a phrase with *than*.

> She was sad last year but she's **happier** now.

Comparative adjectives: Long and irregular forms

FORM

For long adjectives, we form the comparative with *more +* adjective. We don't add *-er*.

> beautiful → *more* beautiful

Some adjectives with two syllables add *-er* for the comparative. Others use *more +* adjective. And some can do either.

> boring → *more* boring
>
> funny → funn*ier*
>
> simple → *more* simple OR simpl*er*

The adjectives *good*, *bad* and *far* are irregular. The comparative form is a different word.

> good → *better*
>
> bad → *worse*
>
> far → *farther* OR *further*

GO ONLINE for the complete grammar reference.

Unit 11

Present continuous: Positive

FORM

Subject + am/are/is + -ing form.

Subject	am/are/is	-ing form	
I	am	reading. watching listening laughing. dancing.	TV. to music.
You	are		
He/She/It	is		
We/You/They	are		

USE

We use the present continuous to talk about actions happening now. We can also use a time expression.

I'm listening to music.   *We're leaving right now.*

We also use the present continuous to talk about the situation now. We often use a time expression to say *when*.

I'm working this week.

Present continuous: Negative

FORM

Subject + am/are/is + not + -ing form.

Subject + *be*	not	-ing form	
I'm	not	reading. watching listening dancing. swimming.	TV. to music.
Subject	**be + not**		
You	aren't		
He/She/It	isn't		
We/You/They	aren't		

USE

We use the negative present continuous to talk about actions not happening now. We also use the negative present continuous with a time expression to talk about the situation now.

They aren't eating lunch.   *She isn't speaking to me today.*

Present continuous: *Yes/no* questions and short answers

FORM

Am/Are/Is + subject + -ing form?

Am/Are/Is	subject	-ing form	
Am	I	reading? waving? making	a cake?
Are	you		
Is	he/she/it		
Are	we/you/they		

Short answers	
Positive (+)	**Negative** (−)
Yes, I *am*.	No, I'm not.
Yes, you *are*.	No, you *aren't*/you're not.
Yes, he/she/it *is*.	No, he/she/it *isn't*.
Yes, we *are*.	No, we *aren't*/we're not.
Yes, they *are*.	No, they *aren't*/they're not.

USE

We use questions in the present continuous to ask about actions happening now.

Are you listening to music?

We also use the present continuous to talk about the situation now. We often use a time expression to say *when*.

"Is he wearing a new coat today?" *"Yes, he is."*

Present continuous: *Wh-* questions

FORM

Question word + am/are/is + subject + -ing form?

Question word	am/are/is	subject	-ing form
What Where Why	am	I	doing? going? laughing?
	are	you	
	is	he/she/it	
	are	we/you/they	

USE

We use the present continuous to ask about actions happening now or the situation now.

What are you doing?   *Where is he going?*

"What are you studying?" *"English and business."*

Using *-ing* forms as subjects

FORM

ing-form + is + adjective/noun

Singing is fun.

Running is awful.

USE

We can use the *ing*-form with the verb *be* to describe activities and talk about our hobbies.

Cooking is boring.   *Watching football is exciting.*

 GO ONLINE for the complete grammar reference.

Unit 12

Superlative adjectives

FORM

For short adjectives, we usually form the superlative with -est.

Short **superlative adjectives**	
add **-est**, or **-st** when the adjective ends in **-e**	tall → tall**est** nice → nice**st**
when the adjective ends in one vowel + one consonant, double the consonant and add **-est**	big → big**gest** hot → hot**test**
change **-y** to **-iest**	happy → happ**iest**

For long adjectives, we form the superlative with *most* + adjective. We don't add -est.

   beautiful → *most* beautiful

Some adjectives with two syllables add -est for the superlative. Others use *most* + adjective. And some can do either.

   boring → *most* boring   funny → funn**iest**
   simple → *most* simple → simpl**est**

The adjectives *good*, *bad* and *far* are irregular. The superlative form is a different word.

   good → *best*   bad → *worst*
   far → *farthest* OR *furthest*

We use *the* before superlative adjectives.

   the smallest animal

USE

We use superlative adjectives to describe how three or more things, animals, or people are different from the group they belong to. We use *the* before superlative adjectives.

   *Chocolate is **the best** ice cream flavor.*

After superlatives, we often use *in* before a group or a place.

   *Ed is **the tallest** boy in my class.*

Going to: Future plans

FORM

Subject + be + going to + infinitive.

Positive (+)			
Subject + **be**	**going to**	**infinitive**	
I**'m**	going to	swim.	
You**'re**		have	fun!

Subject + be + not + going to + infinitive.

Negative (–)			
Subject + **be** + **not**	**going to**	**infinitive**	
You **aren't**	going to	ride	horses.
He/She/It **isn't**		be	a teacher.

USE

We use *be* + *going to* to talk about future plans.

   I'm going to drive to the beach.

We often use *be* + *going to* with future time expressions, e.g. *tomorrow, next week, next year*, etc.

   We're going to ride horses tomorrow.

Going to: Questions

FORM

We form *yes/no* questions with:

Be + subject + going to + infinitive?

Yes/no questions (?)				
Be	**subject**	**going to**	**infinitive**	
Am	I	going to	travel?	
Are	you			
Is	he/she/it		go	to the party?
Are	we/you/they			

We usually answer with a short answer.

   "**Are** you **going to buy** a new phone?"   "No, **I'm not**."

We form *wh-* questions with:

Question word + *be* + subject + *going to* + infinitive?

Wh- questions (?)				
Question word	**be**	**subject**	**going to**	**infinitive**
Where	*are*	you	going to	go?
When	*is*	she		travel?
What	*are*	they		do?

USE

We use *be* + *going to* to ask about future plans.

   "**Where's** he **going to stay**?"   "**He's going to stay** in Rome."

We can answer yes/no questions with a short answer.

   "**Is** he **going to go** to Italy?"   "Yes, **he is**."

We can also answer *wh-* questions with a short answer.

   "**When is** she **going to finish** college?"   "In May."

We often use *be* + *going to* with future time expressions, e.g. *tomorrow, next week, tonight, next year*, etc.

   "**Are** you **going to visit Max** tomorrow?"   "Yes, **I am**."

 GO ONLINE for the complete grammar reference.